On Being Human

On Being Human

Interpretations of Humanism from
The Renaissance to the Present

Salvatore Puledda

Translated by Andrew Hurley

Foreword by Mikhail Gorbachev

New Humanism Series

Latitude Press
San Diego

This book is part of the *New Humanism Series* of contemporary nonfiction and fiction addressing the growing need to humanize both individual life and society in today's world. To obtain a free catalog, additional copies of this book, or other titles in the New Humanism Series, contact Latitude Press at P.O. Box 231516, Encinitas, CA 92023-1516 U.S.A.; 800-LATITUDE (800-528-4883); email 73250.574@compuserve.com; web site www.latitudepress.com.

Latitude Press is committed to publishing important books that reflect a contemporary approach to building a human world at both the individual and community levels, and contributes the the net income from this series to these efforts.

This edition contains the complete unabridged text of this work. Original title: *Interpretaciones del humanismo*. Translated by Andrew Hurley. Foreword translated by Marian Schwartz.

Acknowledgments and permissions too lengthy to appear on this page appear on page 167 as an extension of this copyright page.

LIBRARY OF CONGRESS CATALOGING-IN-PUBLICATION DATA
Puledda, Salvatore, 1943–
        [Interpretaciones del humanismo. English]
        On being human: Interpretations of humanism from the
Renaissance to the present / by Salvatore Puledda; foreword by
Mikhail Gorbachev; translated by Andrew Hurley. – 1st ed.
          p.   cm. – (New humanism series)
        Includes bibliographical references and index.
        ISBN 1–878977–18–0 (pbk.)
        1. Humanism.   I. Title.   II. Series.
B821.P8513   1997
144–dc20   96–32530
                                           CIP

Published by Latitude Press.

Printed in the U.S.A. on acid-free recycled paper meeting the guidelines of the Committee on Production Guidelines for Book Longevity of the Council on Library Resources.

First Edition
A B C D E

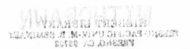

Contents

Foreword

A Prerequisite for Survival

YOU HAVE before you a book, *On Being Human,* that will certainly cause you to think, not only because it is devoted to the timeless topic of humanism, but also because, by setting this topic in its historical context, this book can help you see how a new humanism is the most valid approach to facing the key challenges of our time.

The author, Salvatore Puledda, rightly notes that humanism, in concept and content as well as in the actions it inspires, has a long and richly complex history that has ebbed and flowed like the oceans' tides, at times coming to the fore and occupying center stage in the history of humanity and then at other times seeming to "vanish."

Not that humanism has ever actually vanished altogether. Rather, it has simply been pushed into the background by those forces that noted author on humanism Mario Rodríguez Cobos (Silo) quite properly characterizes as "anti-humanist." And during such periods of eclipse it has often been subjected to the most crude distortions. Anti-humanist forces have frequently donned a mask of humanism in order to pursue their monstrous deeds under its cover and even in its name. Yet despite this, the true idea of humanism has persisted somewhere deep in human consciousness and in the minds of our best thinkers as an ideal, a goal, a desirable direction for social endeavor.

Dr. Puledda is certainly correct when he asserts that humanism, both past and present, has been subject to myriad and even quite contradictory interpretations. Furthermore, different types of readers will likely perceive the content of this book in different ways, depending on whether they agree or disagree with its conclusions. In fact – and this is an important characteristic of the work – Dr. Puledda does not claim that he possesses the ultimate truth; he reasons and invites the reader to reason with him.

As for me, I am convinced that *On Being Human* is a book that is both timely and relevant. It is my belief, as well as that of others in the foundation I head, that we are in the throes of a crisis that is shaking the very foundations of modern civilization, in the process nearly exhausting its potential. You could say this is a crisis of the human being, of humanity itself.

Everything that is happening – certainly the greater part of it – seems like nothing so much as an attack on the human being. So many things are arrayed against us: the numerous consequences of the ways that scientific-technical progress is applied (which with other approaches to using its fruits could make life for all people better and more dignified); the related and profound crisis in society's relationship to the rest of nature; upheavals in the sociopolitical sphere; the exacerbated contradictions between the human being and society, between the human being and the powers that be; the impasses reached in developing education and culture. While I could go on, I will instead refer all who are interested in the ideas of contemporary humanism to Silo's *Letters to My Friends: On Social and Personal Crisis in Today's World* (*Cartas a mis amigos*). I recommend this work because it treats these problems in detail, and specifically from the standpoint of a new and authentic humanism; Silo and I share very similar views on the current crisis facing both society and the individual.

The problem of society's relationship to the rest of nature has today reached tragic proportions. The solution to this problem cannot be purely anthropocentric, however, for just as human beings are the highest development of conscious life, they are also at the same time a part of nature. The task, I am convinced, is not to try to ensure society's dominion over nature (as has been proposed for centuries), but instead to create conditions for their harmonious, mutually dependent development. Humanity can secure all it needs from nature only if it sees to nature's needs and helps to restore and maintain the seriously disrupted balance of the biosphere.

Surmounting the crisis that has overtaken civilization, I believe, implies a transition to a new paradigm of human existence, a new civilization based on the importance and dignity of human beings and directed toward the full realization of their most ample characteristics – in other words, a transition to a civilization that is truly humanist, one that not only overcomes the current dangers and threats to the existence of the human family, to the very survival of our species, but also creates the necessary conditions for the dignified existence of current and future generations. It is only a slight exaggeration to say, summing things up in a few words, that we are talking about the need for a humanist "revolution."

Revolution might not seem the appropriate word here if one considers only the way it is perhaps too widely understood today. I will therefore add that we are speaking of revolution by means of evolution, through gradual transformations and reforms, a converging consensus among various currents of thought and action. Naturally, this approach does not obviate the need to resist the forces of antihumanism should they mount a counterattack. In principle, however, a humanist revolution implies humanist means that correspond to its content, for otherwise its very essence would be lost.

Something more is clear as well, I think. A humanist revolution will never come to pass – or will become only another manifestation of anti-humanism – if it takes the form of some imposed "universal leveling" or uniformity, that is, if it leads to stripping individuals, peoples, and nations of their freedom of choice. Silo is entirely correct when he asserts in the sixth letter of *Letters to My Friends* that "humanism is based on freedom of choice."[1] The entire history of humankind, which to this day has largely meant the suppression of freedom of choice, teaches us that it will take a humanist revolution to guarantee this freedom to the human being, to allow room for the intrinsic diversity of human existence.

Over ten years ago in the Soviet Union we undertook the transformations that came to be known as *perestroika,* which were intended to bring about a thorough and multifaceted humanizing of all spheres of life. First and foremost, our task was to accomplish the transition from totalitarianism, by its very nature an anti-humanist regime, to democracy. On the whole I believe we succeeded, although not everything that we planned was able to come to fruition as we wished.

In August 1991, anti-humanist forces, clinging to the old ways, organized a coup attempt, thereby undermining much of what we had contemplated. And what happened in December of that year – the dissolution of the Soviet Union – has carried its successor states down paths that in large part have meant a departure from the values and mission of perestroika. For Russia, then, as well as the other states that came into being through the breakup of the Soviet Union, the task of building a human life for its people remains largely unrealized to this day.

1. Silo, *Letters to My Friends,* 77.

At the level of world politics, from 1985 on we vigorously directed our foreign policy toward facilitating cooperation with other nations in order to humanize the life of the world community, putting an end to confrontation and moving toward the peaceful and constructive collaboration between states and peoples that constitutes the precondition for accomplishing this task. Much was achieved along these lines: of paramount importance, bringing the Cold War to an end and shifting from the nuclear arms race to nuclear disarmament, from relentless accumulation of new types of arms to reducing weapons stockpiles. Explicit standards of human rights were finally recognized on a world level, and the crisis in the relationship between society and the rest of nature was mitigated though not resolved.

In all these areas we still face tasks of enormous magnitude and scope. We have a long way to go if we are to make the life of the world community more human and to overcome the surviving remnants of the confrontational past (and present in many ways as well).

Dr. Puledda is correct when he observes that our era is increasingly marked by an eclipse of traditional humanism. Nonetheless, it seems to me that we have now reached a stage where the age-old lack of humanism can finally be remedied.

The affirmation of a new humanism – a humanism not only of contemplation and compassion but also of action and cooperation – is the fundamental imperative of our time: it is the prerequisite for humanity's survival. In this context, the publication of Dr. Puledda's book is a notable and important event, a contribution to the spiritual struggle to heal the current crisis of civilization and the search for a path of development that corresponds to the essence and needs of the human being.

Mikhail Gorbachev

Preface

WHO ARE WE, these fascinating and restless creatures called human beings? Is there a fixed "human nature" predetermining our lives, or does human existence encompass the freedom to make choices within an ethical dimension – to choose to change the direction of our lives, or to change society as a whole?

These are more than abstract philosophical questions, for as events in our world accelerate in directions hard to foresee, all of us face difficult choices that affect both our own lives and those around us. And agreement about human nature and freedom is far from unanimous – all major political and religious movements have answered these questions in their own, often divergent ways.

In North America, readers are likely most familiar with definitions of humanism associated with debates such as those between evolutionists and creationists, or more generally between science and fundamentalism. In these sometimes heated arguments, humanism typically appears as a rationalist, naturalistic, and secular philosophy.

It is interesting that the debate concerning what it is to be human and humanism is far broader on a world scale. *On Being Human* approaches these questions on two levels that richly interrelate. On one level Puledda proves an open-minded and informative guide on a tour of some of Western civilization's keenest minds as they probe the question, "What is it to be human?" In a very readable survey of such writers as Pico della Mirandola, Marx, Maritain, Sartre, Heidegger, Lévi-Strauss, Foucault and others, the author brings these sometimes intimidating figures to life through primary references that give the reader a firsthand experience of these thinkers grappling with a surprising range of approaches to the central questions of human life. Concluding with more recent proposals, including those of Gorbachev, Frankl, and the New Humanism of Mario Rodríguez Cobos (Silo), the author addresses the need for a new kind of humanism that must be, more than an idea or a philosophy, a *human attitude* in daily life that can resolve the paradox of building a society that embraces diversity while unifying people within a shared sense of their common humanity – a universal human nation.

On Being Human also acts on a second and more personal level by engaging readers in a helpful meditation on their own lives, on how they can be more fully human. Whether implicitly or explicitly, each of us follows inner models of desirable human qualities and behavior, and this book helps us become more aware of the models in our lives. As we think for ourselves anew on these questions, this forms a healthy antidote to today's corrosive cynicism and apathy that deny change is possible for ourselves or society.

A refreshing broadening of traditional discussions on the human condition, *On Being Human* along with the Appendix extend the dialogue beyond today's prevailing and increasingly unquestioned conception of the human being as nothing more than a "biochemical machine," rendered ever less free, ever more insignificant by determining factors. Because this work goes beyond the traditional dialectic that places what it is to be human and humanism at odds with the subjective, with each person's own experience of his or her existence, *On Being Human* is well-placed to stimulate renewed debate on the status and freedom of the human being at the close of the twentieth century.

The Editors

Translator's Note

IN BEGINNING this book, the reader sensitive to issues of gender – as growing numbers of people are – will soon see that in this regard the book's style is not consistent. The problem in question is the long-standing and nearly universal use of the word *man* and the various masculine personal pronouns to indicate all individuals of the human race. While the author, translator, editors, and our respective colleagues have grappled at some length with the problem, we have, unfortunately, not been able to find a satisfactory solution.

Contemporary language itself (and not only English; every European language) resists expressing the ideas that are central to the humanist position, among them that every human being, woman and man, possesses, at least in potential, the supreme value of the whole species. Every language from which this book takes its sources uses a masculine human-noun to designate all the members of the race; every one uses a masculine singular third-person pronoun as the "inclusive." And there are no other nouns and pronouns available: even if one chooses to say "the individual," there is still no gender-inclusive *personal* pronoun.

Faced with this continuing historical, linguistic, and human dilemma, our approach to the problem has been this: when a source such as Sartre or Heidegger uses the word *man* or the masculine inclusive pronoun *he*, the book simply quotes that source without attempting to "amend" history. Similarly, in speaking generally of the Renaissance, for instance, which tended to use those forms habitually, or when directly commenting on or summarizing a passage that has used one of the masculine-inclusive forms, this book may simply continue to use that form. But whenever it is *logically possible* to summarize a source in more gender-inclusive forms, or when it is the author, Salvatore Puledda, who is speaking about the human race and the individual members who comprise it, then the book uses *humankind, humanity, the human being,* and so forth, or sometimes the more personal locution he or she / him or her and its related forms. Thus, there are two languages, and no doubt two realities, at work in this book; therein the seeming stylistic inconsistency.

Ideally, our languages would permit the full inclusion of every member of the human race. But they do not, at least not now, and that, too, must be part of the program of New Humanism.

Introduction

TODAY, the word *humanism* is understood in the most vague and indeterminate ways, and not infrequently it is employed by people of differing viewpoints in contradictory senses. Thus, in this survey I believe it is important to reconstruct the various ways in which the word humanism has been interpreted throughout its history, and to review, at least with respect to their essential features, the historical and philosophical contexts within which these interpretations arose.

Frequently we find the term *humanism* used to indicate any current of thought that affirms the centrality, value, and dignity of the human being or that manifests a primary concern or interest in the life and situation of the human being in the world. Such a broad definition has allowed philosophers and observers to use and interpret the word in a surprising variety of ways, thereby giving rise to considerable confusion and misunderstanding. The designation "humanist" has been adopted by numerous philosophers who – each in his or her own way – have claimed to possess a knowledge of what or who the human being is and of the correct path toward the realization of those potentials that constitute an important part of being human. It is noteworthy that every philosophy that has called itself "humanist" has put forth a conception of the "nature" or "essence" of humanity. From its idea of "human nature," each "humanism" then derives a series of consequences in the sphere of practice, always taking care to point out what human beings should or must do in order to fully manifest their "humanity."

1

When used within a particular historical framework, the word humanism has a second meaning that is more limited and precise. In this case, the word is used to designate the complex and multiform cultural movement that several centuries ago produced a radical transformation of Western civilization and brought to an end the Christian Middle Ages. The fourteenth and fifteenth centuries in Italy, where this fruitful "mutation" began, are known as the Age of Humanism, while the next hundred years, in which this transformation spread like a shock wave across all of Europe, is known as the Renaissance. Used in this context, the word humanism unequivocally indicates that specific cultural movement in the West, its forms and temporal limits historically defined.

In more recent times, a new interpretation, reformulating the concept of humanism and known as *New Humanism,* has appeared. Reflecting the current age, which is beginning to glimpse the first lights of a new and planetary civilization, this line of thought sets the concept of humanism within a historical perspective of global dimensions. It recognizes that the humanism that appeared in Europe during the period called the Renaissance was implicit in other cultures as well, cultures that in fact contributed in decisive ways to the formation of Western civilization. Seen from this perspective, humanism is not a geographically or temporally limited phenomenon but one that has arisen and taken shape at various times and in various parts of the world and that can, precisely for that reason, bring into confluence diverse cultures that now find themselves thrown into contact on a planet made ever smaller and more unified by mass media. Adding weight to that view are the profound direct and historically demonstrable contributions to historical and Renaissance humanism in the West from the cultures of the Middle East and the similarly substantial indirect contributions from the cultures of Asia. For the emerging movement known as New Humanism this is a point of utmost importance, though it is beyond the scope of this work and deserves to be dealt with *in extenso* in a work of its own.[2]

In this work we will begin by examining the aspects of Renaissance humanism that we view as essential to an understanding of its specific historical characteristics and its innovating energies. In this examination we will make a special effort to clarify the meaning of the ideal of *humanitas,* which was the emblem of Renaissance humanism, and we will review the new image of the human being and the natural world that Renaissance humanism constructed in opposition to the image that had prevailed throughout the Middle Ages.

We will then offer brief descriptions of major philosophical currents that have been called humanist in our own century. We will review Marxist, Christian, and existentialist humanisms, as well as humanisms of even more recent coinage such as New Humanism, attempting to cast light on the conception of the human being, explicit or implicit, held by each current. We will also give some space to the points of view of those who have directed radical criticisms against philosophical humanisms or taken programmatically antihumanist positions. The first case is that of Martin Heidegger; the second includes the "structuralists," represented here by the figure of Claude Lévi-Strauss, and also Michel Foucault.

We shall see in the course of this survey that while the philosophical currents of the nineteenth century exhibited a renewed interest in humanism, they arrived at radically divergent interpretations of it. In distinction to the Renaissance, then, in the twentieth century we find not a single uni-

2. See World Center for Humanist Studies. *Anuario 1994 (Yearbook 1994).*

fied current of humanism that is homogeneous in spite of its complexity; what we instead find is conflict among various humanisms, plural. And this is how, as we said at the outset, the meaning of the word has gradually been lost in a confusion of tongues and interpretations.

But the voices of this "Tower of Babel" have suddenly fallen silent. After the pronouncements of the "philosophers of existence" at the end of the 1940s, the debate over humanism apparently faded away. Today few voices (and those largely unheeded) are raised to propose to human beings a new understanding of their "humanity." Indeed, while one hears much talk about "human rights" (often systematically trampled upon), "human nature" (described in vague and contradictory terms), and the proper place of the human being in the natural world (especially in light of the critical environmental problems now facing the world), it is clear that our day is witnessing an eclipse of humanism. This is not surprising, of course; humanist currents, which have appeared since the beginning of Western civilization, have displayed a behavior that is wave-like – appearing in certain periods and later fading from view, only to reappear once again. This is what happened with the humanism of antiquity, which developed in the Greek and Roman schools of philosophy and was then blotted out for ten centuries by medieval Christianity, only to arise once more with great vigor in the Renaissance. Renaissance humanism, in turn, gradually lost impetus until it was displaced by the anti-humanistic philosophies of recent centuries. If this is the way things are, then surely it is not utopian to anticipate the resurgence of a new current of humanism able to counteract the crisis of our own age, which includes our loss of the sense of what it is to be human – a crisis made all the worse by the prospect of global catastrophe in all its terrifying aspects.

Renaissance Humanism

1. The Return to the Ancients and the Ideal of *Humanitas*

THE REMARKABLE phenomenon known as Renaissance humanism emerged and flowered for a brief interval extending from the second half of the fourteenth century to the end of the sixteenth. First in Italy and then all across Europe, this was a time of extraordinary historical dynamism, in which radical political and spiritual transformations succeeded one another at a dizzying pace.

A subject of endless debate among historians is whether this humanism constitutes a complete break with the Middle Ages or is instead the culmination of philosophical, religious, social, economic, and other tendencies that had already appeared in the late Middle Ages. There are undoubtedly excellent arguments on both sides, but whichever position one may choose to take, no historical reconstruction can afford to overlook the image that the protagonists of that time held of their age or the meaning they attributed to the works they were producing. Upon this point there can be no ambiguity because the assessment was unanimous: all the great figures of humanism perceived the time in which they were living as "special" – a time in which humanity, emerging from the long sleep of barbarism in the Middle Ages, was returning to its origins and passing through a "renaissance," understood as the mystical tradition defined that word – that is, a "second birth," an all-encompassing renewal that would allow humanity to recover the strength and energy that were to be found only in "the beginning." Therefore, for the culture of humanism[3] it was not a question of further developing or bringing to completion elements of the preceding age but instead constructing a *completely new* world, a *completely new* humanity, and that task, in keeping with the image of "rebirth," was possible only through death – the death or disappearance of the medieval world and medieval man.

For the Christian Middle Ages the world was the locus of sin and suffering, a vale of tears into which the sin of Adam had cast humanity; humankind was to shun and flee the things of this world. Humanity was nothing and could do nothing for itself; its worldly desires were madness and vain ambition, its works but dust; all that could be hoped for was the forgiveness of a God who was infinitely remote in His perfection and transcendence and whose grace was granted in inscrutable ways.

The image of the universe in the Middle Ages was a reflection of that theological vision. The Earth, according to Ptolemaic cosmology, was an immobile body fixed at the center of the universe; it was surrounded by the spheres of the sun and the planets, revolving under the impulse of angelic hands, and beyond those, the sphere of the fixed stars. In that universe's highest heaven, the empyrean, was the throne of God, the Unmoved Mover of all. In turn, the medieval conception of history reflected that determinedly hierar-

---

3. The term *humanism* was coined at a relatively recent date, introduced (as "Humanismus") by the German educator F. J. Niethammer in the early nineteenth century to indicate the importance given the study of Greek and Latin language and literature in the German secondary schools of that time. The Latin word *humanista* appeared in Italy during the first half of the sixteenth century, with the meaning "a man of letters who dedicates himself to the *studia humanitatis.*" See Kristeller, *Renaissance Thought and Its Sources,* 21–22. See also Kristeller, *Renaissance Thought: The Classic, Scholastic, and Humanistic Strains,* 8–10, 120–23.

chical and theonomous view. History was not the memory of men and women, peoples, and civilizations, but rather the path of expiation that led from original sin to redemption. Finally, at the end of time, following the awful cataclysms of the Apocalypse, would come the terrible judgment of God.

The social organization of the Middle Ages mirrored this vision of a closed and hierarchical universe. The sphere of the nobility was kept rigidly separate from the subordinate classes of the bourgeoisie and serfs, and the "place" of an individual was perpetuated hereditarily. At the apex of power stood the two shepherds of the Christian flock, the Pope and the Emperor, sometimes allied, sometimes locked in fierce struggle for preeminence in that hierarchy. The economic structure followed the same pattern: the economy of the Middle Ages, until at least the eleventh century, was a closed system based on the consumption of products at the place of their production.

The culture of humanism totally rejected the medieval vision of the world, and in its effort to construct a completely renewed humanity and world took as its model the classical civilizations of Greece and Rome. Thus, the return to the beginning, the "rebirth" or "renaissance," was a return to the ancients, a rescuing of the experience of a civilization to which were attributed those first, "original" potentialities of humanity that the Christian Middle Ages had destroyed, denied, or forgotten.

In its beginnings, humanism manifested itself above all as a *literary* phenomenon, a rediscovery of the texts and culture of classical antiquity. The search for ancient manuscripts, buried and forgotten in convent and monastery libraries, began with Petrarch (1304–1374). Only one hundred years later, almost ten times more was known of the Roman world than had been known for a millennium. In addition, the arrival in Italy of two waves of scholars from Byzantium – the first in 1439 on the occasion of the Council of Florence (intended to sanction the reunification of the Orthodox and Roman churches), and the second in 1453 with the fall of Constantinople – brought an influx of new knowledge of the Greek world to the West.

The literature of Greece and Rome that thereby came to light was an *earthly* literature. It was a literature that spoke of the men and women of this world, radically different from the Christian literature of sacred books, the fathers of the Church, and medieval doctors, in which God and the ultramundane life are the only subjects of interest. It was in this contrast between the *humanæ litteræ* and the *divinæ litteræ* that the cultural renewal brought about by humanism had its real beginning. Clearly, however, the ancient texts would have served for little had not European society been capable of seeing those vestiges of the ancient world with new eyes and a renewed curiosity. Indeed, in the humanists one immediately perceives a new attitude toward the works of literature that were discovered.

First and foremost, one sees a love for the text itself, which humanists attempted to reconstruct in its original form, freed from the interpolations and distortions inserted by generations of clerics intent upon adapting it to the Christian view of the universe. The great discovery that is associated with this attitude (and that goes hand in hand with the introduction of optical perspective in painting) is *historical perspective:* the classical text, faithfully reconstructed, allowed humanists to perceive with full clarity the impossibility of reconciling the Greco-Roman world with that of medieval Christianity. For these humanists, therefore, the awareness of the difference between past and present became an awareness of the flux of history, a phenomenon that the medieval vision of the world had simply blotted out.

Moreover, the rediscovered ancient texts presented an extraordinary range of strong individual human beings oriented toward action, neither fleeing the world nor holding it in contempt, but instead living within human society, feeling a commitment to it, and struggling to shape their own destinies. These individuals became models for the person of the Renaissance to follow, for their way of life seemed best suited to meeting the needs and satisfying the aspirations of a society in rapid transformation, one that deeply felt the need to create new ways of organizing its life and new instruments with which to master nature.

But the culture of humanism cannot be reduced to an artificial imitation of the models of the past. On the contrary, its vitality lay precisely in its recognition that a return to the great examples of antiquity would be utterly futile if a redirection of moral, artistic, religious, and political life were not the result. For the culture of humanism, imitating the ancients meant above all to *educate* the new person as the ancients had done, cultivating those "virtues" they had shown themselves to possess in the highest degree and had expressed in their civic life. It was only with individuals educated in this way that would it truly be possible to renew human society.

Thus, Renaissance humanism took as its own that simultaneously political and educational ideal that figures such as Cicero and Varro had advocated in Rome during the period of the Republic: the ideal of *humanitas,* the Latin translation of the Greek word *paideia,* "education." In a confluence rich in meanings, *humanitas* came to indicate the formation and development, through education, of those qualities that make an individual a truly *human* being, that rescue "humanity" from its natural condition and differentiate it from the barbarian. With the concept of *humanitas* the Romans wished to denote a cultural operation: the construction of the individual, the citizen, who lives and acts within human society.

The instrument employed by this first Western "humanism" in Rome was Greek culture, which the Roman world of the first century B.C. found systematized in the curricula of the philosophical schools of the late Hellenic period. Flourishing after the creative period of Greek philosophy had already waned, these schools were eclectic in orientation. However, the Roman world was able to take from them the themes, methods of investigation, and language that had been developed in the classical philosophical systems, and Rome's encounter with Greek culture quickly blossomed into that splendid flowering of Latin literature that took place in the last century B.C. and the first of the Christian era. It was in institutions of this kind and under the example of figures such as Cicero that the new Roman intellectual and political class was educated, assimilating a body of philosophical knowledge and a poetic and artistic culture that had previously been almost completely overlooked in Roman traditions more focused on such themes as jurisprudence, military organization, and engineering.

Thus, after almost ten centuries of Christian culture there reappeared in the West the ideal of *humanitas,* that confidence in the immense formative power that philosophy, poetry, and the arts exercise on the human personality, a confidence characteristic first of Greece and later of Rome, and in which we can identify the very essence of Renaissance humanism. Education was now imparted through the great classics of Latin literature and secondarily, given the limited knowledge of the language, through the classics of Greece. It was those texts, that curriculum, upon which were based the *studia humanitatis,* and thus the name *humanista* was applied to scholars who devoted themselves to those studies which, in the early fifteenth century in Italy, included grammar, rhetoric, poetry, history, and moral philosophy.

Nevertheless, one must always bear in mind that for the humanism of the Renaissance, these disciplines were not a mere course of studies that transmitted a body of ideas and formulas. On the contrary, the *studia humanitatis* were fundamentally a vehicle for educating the personality, for developing human freedom, creativity, and all those qualities that were seen to allow human beings to live happily and honorably in society. In that sense, humanists were not only scholars or men of letters, but the protagonists of a great project of moral, cultural, and political transformation, a project whose motto, *Iuvat vivere* (It is pleasant to live), is witness to the optimism, the sense of freedom and liberty, and the renewed love of life that characterized the age.

2. The New Image of Man

Every text and every aspect of the literature of humanism was aimed toward the exaltation of humanity and the reaffirmation of human dignity, in opposition to the devaluation of the human being in the Christian Middle Ages. No matter how diverse the themes and subjects of the literature of humanism, all pointed to one common objective: the recovery of faith in the creativity of humankind and in humanity's capacity to transform the world and to forge its own destiny.

Humanism's attack on the medieval conception of the world was constant and determined: in his 1452 work "On the Dignity of Man" (*De dignitate et excellentia hominis*), Gianozzo Manetti (1396–1459), one of humanism's first major figures, criticized that work perhaps most representative of the medieval mentality, "On the Misery of the Human Condition" (*De miseria condicionis humanæ*)[4] by Lothar of Segni who was later to become Pope Innocent III (r. 1198–1216), one of the most powerful popes of the Middle Ages. In opposition to Lothar's view of the wretchedness and degradation of human nature (which left the individual easy prey to vice and sinfulness) and the weakness of the human body, Manetti exalted the whole of the human physical and moral being. He praised the proportions of the human body, its harmonious workings as a physical organism, the excellence of human wit and ingenuity, the beauty of humanity's works, the daring and audacity of human undertakings. Humankind's great voyages, the conquest of the seas, the wonders of works of art, science, literature, law – these things constituted the world of the human spirit, the kingdom that humankind had built for itself out of its own genius. Nor in Manetti's view did humanity live upon the Earth as a simple inhabitant, one creature among many; instead, God had assigned to humanity a privileged place, creating beings with their heads held high so that they might contemplate the heavens and be spectators of the highest realities of the universe. At the center of Manetti's philosophy was human freedom, which was not simply a gift from God but a daily labor through which humankind brings beauty and perfection to the wonders of creation. Thus, a human being was not a helpless and contemptible creature but a free collaborator with divinity itself.

Another of humanism's early great figures was Lorenzo Valla (1407–1457), whose dialogue "On Pleasure" (*De voluptate*, c1430) attacked one of the key points of the medieval ethos, the rejection of the body and its pleasure. Starting with Epicurean ideas, which the rediscovery of Lucretius'

---

4. See Sayers, *Innocent III*, or Packard, *Europe and the Church under Innocent III*.

work had once more made available, Valla launched a harsh diatribe against all moral asceticism, whether Stoic or Christian, that would lead the individual to disdain the body and to reject pleasure. For Valla, all human actions, even those that appeared to derive from other motives, were inspired by hedonistic ends. Valla saw even the aspiration toward a life after death as within this one overarching aim. For what could be more hedonistic, Valla asked, than the heavenly life that the Scriptures themselves called a *paradisus voluptatis*, a "paradise of pleasure"? There could be no dichotomy between the body and the spirit, no *a priori* "good" part and "bad" part of the human being. Pleasure, far from being a sin, was rather a divine gift, *divina voluptas*. In pleasure, Nature expressed itself in all its vigor, and in the way most fitting for itself. Inverting the usual terms of the debate, Valla declared that the real sin lay in demeaning and repressing the nature that throbs and lives within us, in shunning physical love and beauty. Therefore, Valla's hymn to happiness, exalting *all* of the person, offered not only to heal the old dualism between the flesh and the spirit but also to supplant the pessimism of the ancient Epicureans.

Leon Battista Alberti (1404–1472) – philosopher, mathematician, musician, architect – was one of those extraordinary universal personalities that the age of the Renaissance lavished upon the world. At the center of Alberti's reflections was one of humanism's most characteristic ideas: that human actions are able to conquer even Fate itself. In the prologue to his famous work "On the Family" (*Della Famiglia*), Alberti denied the ascetic life any value, rejected all pessimistic views of humankind, and accorded the highest dignity to human action. Humanity's true greatness, Alberti argued, lies in labor, which allows the family and the city to grow and to thrive. Alberti turned on its head the medieval ethic of poverty and self-abnegation, declaring that the flourishing of wealth and earthly possessions was not only *not* in conflict with religious principles, but indeed was a clear and tangible expression of divine favor. Moreover, "virtue," understood as strength of will and capacity for doing and as human labor (in the social and political spheres as well as in field or workshop), was superior to Fate itself. In Alberti's view, a man was the cause of his own "fortune" and "misfortune." Only the ignorant and stupid blamed Fate as the origin of their adversity. Fate, or "fortune," could never totally limit or determine human action when that action was truly virtuous. And if Fate sometimes appeared not to reward virtue or even to overwhelm it, the defeat was only temporary and might have its educational and creative function.

In Alberti's scheme, therefore, there was no place for withdrawal from the world, or for an individual's submission to Fate. Quite the contrary: true human dignity manifested itself in human transformation of nature and society. Alberti, a great architectural innovator and theorist of architecture, yearned to build the ideal city (another constant motif in humanist thought), in which Nature would be subject to the intentions of Art. The ideal city, made by and for humankind and in accordance with harmonic geometric structures, would be not only the locus of human action but also the place where, through the exercise of social virtues, God's true glorification would be possible.

Here we see clearly the same great motifs present since the first Renaissance humanists: the exaltation of humankind and human creative capacities and the break with the medieval ethos. By the end of the fifteenth century, with the rediscovery of Platonic philosophy and the Hermetic doctrines, the image of the human being was projected into a religious dimension and humanity acquired a cosmic value.

A principal protagonist in the Renaissance Neoplatonist movement and a central figure in the Florentine Academy, Marsilio Ficino (1433–1499) was one of the great Italian humanists of the time. Under the patronage of Cosimo de' Medici (father of Lorenzo the Magnificent), Ficino translated into Latin all the works of Plato and Plotinus and several works by the Neoplatonists of antiquity. Ficino's most important contribution to the construction of Renaissance philosophical thought, however, was his translation of the *Hermetica* (*Corpus Hermeticum*), that body of works containing the teachings of the legendary philosopher Hermes Trismegistus, "Thrice-Great Hermes." The manuscripts of what became known as the "Hermetic texts" were introduced to the West thanks to Cosimo's interest in – one might even say passion for – ancient texts, as he dispatched agents throughout the Byzantine Empire to search out and purchase ancient codices.

The exceptional importance that Cosimo and the rest of the humanistic world attached to these works can be appreciated if we consider that Cosimo ordered Ficino to put aside his translation of Plato to work on Trismegistus – that is, the wisdom taught by Trismegistus was considered greater even than that of the "divine" Plato. The figure of Hermes Trismegistus became so popular that his portrait can be found beside Moses in the great mosaic at the entrance to the Cathedral of Siena.

The Hermetic texts, which contain philosophical teachings mixed with magical and alchemical formulas, are believed by modern criticism to have been written between the second century B.C. and the third century A.D., and to be the expression of syncretic Greco-Egyptian influences, although the possibility that they transmit much more ancient teachings cannot be excluded.[5] Ficino and his contemporaries attributed great antiquity to these texts, believing that in them they had rediscovered the religion of ancient Egypt or even the original religion of humanity, which had been passed down to Moses and the great figures of the pagan and Christian world – Zarathustra, Orpheus, Pythagoras, Plato, and Augustine. Ficino came to believe that a form of natural religion had existed at all times in all peoples, taking on different forms or guises in different ages and in the different nations.[6] This view helped address two religious issues felt at the time to be crucial: the reconciliation of distinct religions (especially Christianity and Islam) and the question of how Divine Providence could operate for those peoples who for historical and geographical reasons had not known the gospel of Christ. Thus, Christianity was recast as a historical religion, neither the first nor the last, but rather one manifestation of humanity's primitive religion. Moreover, the true roots of Christianity were to be sought in that primordial religion and not in the barbaric forms of the medieval Church.

Ficino is a complex figure in Renaissance philosophy; his paramount concern was to reconcile the dignity and freedom of the human being, extolled since the beginnings of the humanist movement, with the problem of religion, which humanism had not adequately addressed. He was at once the most determined disseminator of Platonism and a staunch adherent of Christianity – even taking religious orders – for in his view Christianity and Platonism shared a single profound essence. Thus, taking as his point of departure the ground of religion, Ficino completed the work of glorifica-

5. See Doresse, *Histoire des religions.*
6. See Yates, *Giordano Bruno and the Hermetic Tradition,* chaps. 1–4.

tion of human nature begun by the first humanists, elevating humanity almost to the level of a god.

From the Neoplatonists of antiquity Ficino took the idea that the divine, the One, manifested itself through successive emanations onto every plane of being. There was therefore, Ficino argued, no break, no abyss, between man and nature on the one hand and God on the other, but rather an uninterrupted passage from God to angels, from angels to mankind, and thence downward to animals, plants, and minerals. Human beings were at the center of the Great Chain of Being, the link between that which is eternal and that which exists in time. The human soul, midpoint and mirror of all things, could contain within itself the entire universe.

Here is how Ficino expresses this idea in his work *Platonic Theology* (*Theologia Platonica,* 1482) (XIV, 3):

> Does not the soul try to become everything just as God is everything? It does in a wonderful way; for the soul lives the life of a plant when it serves the body in feeding it; the life of an animal, when it flatters the senses; the life of a man, when it deliberates through reason on human affairs; the life of the heroes, when it investigates natural things; the life of the dæmons, when it speculates on mathematics; the life of the angels, when it enquires into the divine mysteries; the life of God, when it does everything for God's sake. Every man's soul experiences all these things in itself in some way, although different souls do it in different ways, and thus the human species strives to become all things by living the lives of all things. This is what Hermes Trismegistus was admiring when he said: Man is a great miracle.[7]

It was this same maxim, attributed to Trismegistus, that Giovanni Pico della Mirandola (1463–1494), one of the most remarkable figures in the history of humanism, cited at

---

7. Ficino, *Platonic Theology,* 235–36.

the beginning of his famous work *Oration on the Dignity of Man* (*Oratio de hominis dignitate*, 1486). Given the propagandistic purposes for which it was written, it might well be considered a true "humanist manifesto."

Pico belonged to a wealthy family of the nobility, and even as a very young man had shown extraordinary powers of mind and intellectual curiosity. He knew Greek, Arabic, Hebrew, and Aramaic, studied the great Muslim and Jewish philosophers, and was fascinated by the Kabbalah, mystical teachings based on esoteric interpretations of the Hebrew Scriptures. At the age of twenty-four he attempted to gather together and produce a synthesis of all the wisdom of his time, and he generated a work of nine hundred theses that he intended to have publicly debated in Rome by the wisest men of the age, who would be brought together from the four corners of the earth at Pico's own expense. But this extraordinary program, which was to bridge religions and cultures and was put forth as a means of securing peace and reconciliation, encountered the immediate opposition of the Church, which found thirteen of the theses to be heretical, and so the great debate was forbidden. Pico himself fled to Paris, where he was arrested on orders of the Pope. His life was spared only because of the sympathy he had earned at the French court and in the intellectual circles of the time. A short time afterward Pico took refuge in Florence, where under the protection of Lorenzo the Magnificent he spent the rest of his short life.

Oration on the Dignity of Man was conceived as an oration to be read at the opening of the projected great debate in Rome, in order to give direction to the event and define its scope. At its beginning, Pico presents his conception of the human being, doing so with a rhetorical figure of great effectiveness: God explaining how He has created man. Here is the relevant text:

"We have given thee, Adam, no fixed seat, no form of thy very own, no gift peculiarly thine, that thou mayest feel as thine own, have as thine own, possess as thine own the seat, the form, the gifts which thou thyself shalt desire. A limited nature in other creatures is confined within the laws written down by Us. In conformity with thy free judgment, in whose hands I have placed thee, thou art confined by no bounds; and thou wilt fix limits of nature for thyself. I have placed thee at the center of the world, that from there thou mayest more conveniently look around and see whatsoever is in the world. Neither heavenly nor earthly, neither mortal nor immortal have We made thee. Thou, like a judge appointed for being honorable, art the molder and maker of thyself; thou mayest sculpt thyself into whatever shape thou dost prefer. Thou canst grow downward into the lower natures which are brutes. Thou canst again grow upward from thy soul's reason into the higher natures which are divine."[8]

For Pico, then, human beings had no rigidly fixed "nature" to condition or determine their actions as do other creatures of nature. To be human was fundamentally to live in the *absence* of constraint – in the presence of freedom and choice. A man might be all things; by his free choice he might set himself at any level of being, might lower himself to live like an animal or raise himself to a state in which he would participate in the divine life. Human beings were, therefore, pure existence, constructing themselves through the exercise of choice.

It is difficult to overestimate the importance of this conception of the human being, so clearly expressed in this essay, or the influence it has exercised, directly or indirectly, down through history to our own times. It is a conception that breaks the bonds of any determinism and situates the essence of the human being on the plane of freedom.

8. Pico della Mirandola, *Oration on the Dignity of Man*, 4–5.

It was in "The Wise Man" (*De Sapiente*) by French humanist Carolus Bovillus (Charles de Bouelles) (1479–1567), that the glorification of humankind reached perhaps its maximum expression. Following Ficino and Pico, in whose philosophy he had been schooled, Bovillus declared that human beings did not possess a specific or fixed nature, that indeed they actually subsumed within themselves all degrees of existence: human beings had an existence (*esse*) like that of inanimate matter, lived (*vivere*) as plants did, felt (*sentire*) as animals did, and in addition reasoned and reflected (*intelligere*). In these manifold capacities the human being resembled creative Nature itself. But not all individuals would be capable of reaching this level; only those who were *wise* might do so, by means of a patient labor of self-construction carried out through virtue (*virtus*) and art (*ars*). Here we can see with great clarity the human ideal that the culture of humanism had always sought: *the superior man*, able to rise above the "nature" of the common man, to construct through choice and struggle a second and higher "nature," a nature closer to that of the divine.[9] This self-construction is a possibility that exists within the human being, just as there exists the possibility of remaining at a lower level of existence.

Bovillus employs and at the same time transcends the microcosm/macrocosm equivalence so characteristic of Hermetic thought. The cosmos, Bovillus said, *was* all but *was not aware of what it was;* humankind *was* almost nothing but *could know* all things. Between humankind and the world was the same relationship as between the soul and the body: the human being was the soul of the world, and the

9. The Hermetic motif of the "superior man," who makes himself and rises above the common level of humanity, brings the ideas of European humanism into congruence with those of other traditional philosophies, such as Sufism and Hinduism, among others.

world was the body of the human being. But the self-consciousness that humankind brings to the world, a sort of "humanization of the world," sets humanity *above* the world.[10] The supreme value this conception attributes to the human being could well lead us to consider Bovillus's work as "the worthy epigraph of the philosophy of humanism."[11]

3. The New Image of the World

During the Renaissance, every philosophical current of the age was permeated with "naturalism," though the term was not then used in today's sense and had a special connotation unlike – in fact incompatible with – its modern meaning.

The natural world was not, as in the present-day scientific view, pure inanimate matter subject to blind mechanical laws, but rather a living organism imbued with energies that greatly resembled the energies of the human being. The universe was crisscrossed with infinite currents of thought and sensation, sometimes intertwining and merging, sometimes clashing. Like a person, the world was endowed with senses and intellect, could feel sympathies and antipathies, pleasure and pain. Hermetic thought, on which this conception of the universe was based, saw the world as a gigantic being endowed with an invisible soul – the *world-soul* – which could feel and know, and a visible body composed, like a person's, of various organs and parts. The universe was, then, a *macroanthropos,* as the human being was a *microcosmos.*

And for that reason, the key to deciphering, arriving at an understanding of, the natural world, lay in *the human being*

10. For this formulation of the ideas of Bovillus the author is indebted to the discussion in Cassirer, *The Individual and the Cosmos in Renaissance Philosophy,* 88–92.

11. Ruggiero, *Storia della filosofia, Rinascimento, riforma e controriforma,* 1:126.

itself. The human being was the code for, the paradigm of
the universe, since, as *microcosm,* the human being presented the same fundamental characteristics as that universe.
The structure, the harmony of the human body, the fact that
all its parts were interrelated and carried out complementary
functions – all this was reflected in the solidarity and unity
of the universe. The various planes of being into which the
universe was articulated – minerals, plants, animals, human
beings, the higher intelligences – were neither separate nor
mutually unknown; they were joined by subtle threads, mysterious *correspondences.* In spite of their diversity and the
distance that separated them, star was linked to stone, stone
to plant, plant again to star by a profound and essential relation, a relation that might be even more profound than that
between stone and stone, plant and plant, star and star, for
each thing, on its own plane, was the manifestation of an
ideal form; each was the *sign* of an essential aspect of nature.

Because humanity comprehended within itself all the
planes of being, because of its protean nature, its marvelous
synthesis of all the parts and elements of nature, it was able
to follow the mysterious threads that stretched all across the
Universe from one extreme to the other, and to discover the
secret influences that joined remote and apparently distinct
beings. Humanity might read in nature the signs written by
the hand of God, as though they were the letters of the sacred book of creation.

And if the soul and the intellect acted intentionally upon
the human body, why should they not also act upon the
body of the world of which the human body was an extension? If the moon made the waters rise, if a magnet attracted
iron, if acids ate away metals, why could not a man, who
was all these things at once, act upon every aspect of nature?
He was, after all, able to *know* the hatreds and loves, the
attractions and repulsions that joined or separated the ele-

ments. And while those other forces acted unconsciously, the human being was able to use and master them consciously.

The humanism of the Renaissance, then, conceived the relationship between humanity – in this case, the superior man, the wise man – and nature as basically an animistic or magical one. The wise man was a wizard, a sorcerer, a magician who, by using his intellectual and spiritual faculties, might bend the forces of nature to his own will or cooperate with them. His "art" could speed up, slow down, or transform the processes of nature, to whose secrets he was privy. And indeed, astrology, alchemy, "natural magic" were the "sciences" characteristic of the Renaissance.

It is true, of course, that astrology contained strong elements of determinism and fatalism, and as such it was fiercely combated by Pico, who was much more favorably disposed to magic. If the destiny of individuals, nations, and entire civilizations was dictated by the movements of the stars – motions that subtly determined the individual's behavior – then there was no place for freedom in the great machinery of the Universe. But even the astrological notions of humanism were true to the spirit of the age, and even in astrology the human being and human freedom were placed in the foreground: a knowledge of astral influences was understood as the beginning of liberation from the enslavement that the stars imposed and, with respect to the cosmic plane, lent proof of the oneness of the Universe.

The science of the stars and the laws of nature implied the use of mathematics, though the use of mathematics in the sciences of the Renaissance was quite different from its use in modern science. Faithful to the ideas of Pythagoras and Plato, the humanism of the Renaissance conceived numbers and geometric figures not merely as tools to be used in calculation or measurement but as entities in and of themselves, expressions of the most profound truth, symbols of the rationality of the Universe, and comprehensible through humankind's most characteristic faculty: the intellect. Thus, the humanist Luca Pacioli, who rediscovered the "divine proportion," or "golden section," could make mathematics the foundation of all things in the physical and spiritual world, as Pythagoras and Plato had. Mathematics was, then, a *mystical* discipline, not a science whose legitimacy was posited only upon its measuring, predictive, or constructive utility.

Nonetheless, these latter aspects of mathematics were also of fundamental importance in the Renaissance. Individuals of the Renaissance were above all *active:* driven by a need to seek out the truth, the roots of things, they debated and subjected to verification all the certainties that the traditions of the centuries had held sacred – they sought proofs, they probed, they experimented, they built. This spirit of freedom, of openness, of questioning set the condition for the Copernican revolution and all the great discoveries of the age. But at the foundation of technical or scientific labor, of "art" as it was then called, there was also the idea of a natural world not opposed to the human being but in fact the human being's extension. Thus, the attitude toward mathematical and technical matters held by Alberti, Piero della Francesca, and Leonardo, all of whom made vigorous use of mathematics and technology, was substantially different from that of the modern scientist. The distinctions that we make today between alchemy and chemistry, astrology and astronomy, natural magic and science, were unknown in the Renaissance; these lines were drawn only later. Even Newton, at the "late date" of the eighteenth century, wrote a voluminous treatise on alchemy, and further examples of this sort are not hard to find.

For the humanism of the Renaissance there existed within nature a mathematical order that could be discovered and reproduced, but that was at the same time a *divine* order, and reconstructing it through art meant aspiring to, approaching, acting as God, the creator of beautiful things.

By the end of the brief span in which Renaissance humanism flourished in all its spectacular vigor, the new vision of the world and human beings it launched had displaced the medieval vision. And though the legacy of this flowering of humanism has been profound and long-lasting, by the end of the seventeenth century, as before in humanism's wave-like trajectory, its more visible manifestations had submerged out of sight once again. We move forward in our survey, then, to the appearance of more recent Western formulations and debates regarding humanism, which emerge in the nineteenth and especially the twentieth centuries.

Twentieth-Century Humanism

1. Marxist Humanism

IN THE YEARS following World War II, having shown with Stalin the face of an inhuman dictatorship, the model of Marxism that Lenin had established in the Soviet Union entered a dramatic and profound crisis. It was in this context that a new interpretation of Marx's thought arose, in opposition and as an alternative to the "official" Marxism of the Soviet regime. This new line of thought was known as "Marxist humanism." Its exponents held that Marxism had a "human face," that its central concern was, in fact, the liberation of humankind from all forms of oppression and alienation and, consequently, that it was in essence a form of humanism. This line of thought was developed by a rather heterogeneous group of philosophers, among them Ernst Bloch in Germany, Adam Shaff in Poland, Roger Garaudy in France, Rodolfo Mondolfo in Italy, and Erich Fromm and Herbert Marcuse in the United States.

Thus, beginning in the fifties, with the gauntlet that Marxist humanism had flung down (at the level of theoretical reinterpretation) against the "orthodox" doctrine of the Soviet Union, a heated confrontation arose between those two mutually exclusive ways of understanding Marx's thought. This situation was not new, however, not some anomaly in the history of Marxism; on the contrary, it was virtually a constant, for the history of Marxist philosophy and practice has been, for a number of reasons, a history that has known a wide variety of interpretations.

27

In the years immediately following the death of Marx (1818–1883), which saw the Second Congress of the Communist International (1889), Marxism was generally interpreted as a "historical materialism." Historical materialism was understood to be a "scientific" doctrine of human societies and the transformations of those societies; it was widely held to be based on economic facts and was framed within the broad context of a philosophy of the evolution of nature, as conceived by Friedrich Engels (1820–1895). This reading of Marxism was colored by the cultural climate of the time, which was dominated by Darwinism and, more generally, positivism: the "scientific" nature that Marxism claimed for itself was that of the empirical sciences, whose method and rigor it pretended to extend to the realms of economics, sociology, and history that had previously been dominated by "metaphysical," that is, irrational and arbitrary, systems of ideas.

In the twentieth century, the triumph of the proletarian revolution in Russia, paralleled by its failure in Germany and the rest of Western Europe, meant that the model of Marxism that came to prevail was that based on the interpretations of Plekhanov and Lenin (1870–1924), and later Stalin (1879–1953). This view took Marxism to be basically a "dialectical materialism," that is to say, a materialist philosophical doctrine (one might almost say a cosmology) in which dialectics – the logical procedure formulated by Hegel – played a central role. Dialectical materialism was at one and the same time the evolutionary law of matter and the theoretical and practical method that allowed one to understand the physical world and history, and therefore gave one the knowledge that enabled one to choose appropriate political action.

Here, the philosophy of nature formulated by Engels, which in the preceding interpretation had constituted only the philosophical framework for Marx's sociological and philosophical ideas, became central and was superimposed upon Marx's historical materialism. In this case, too, Marxism was understood as a "science," but not in the sense of a discipline that is strictly experimental; it was seen, rather, as a *philosophical science,* which was considered to be "superior" to those other sciences because it was based on the application of the laws of Hegelian dialectics to natural phenomena, and therefore integrated and went beyond the empirical sciences. With Stalin, dialectical materialism became the official doctrine of the Marxist-Leninist party in the Soviet Union and of the Communist parties within its sphere of influence.

Let us now examine the ideas on which these two historically most important interpretations of Marxism, *historical materialism* and *dialectical materialism,* are based. The term historical materialism began to appear in Engels' later works, although he seems to have preferred the expression *materialist conception of history.* When one spoke of historical materialism one generally referred to the analysis and interpretation of human societies and their evolution. The basic thesis underlying this term, enunciated by Marx and Engels in several works, was that those human productions generally thought of as "spiritual" – law, art, philosophy, religion – are *in the final analysis* determined by the economic structure of the societies within which they occur. For Marx, the basic historical datum was the production of the material goods that make possible the survival of individuals and the species. In order to make history, human beings had first of all to manage to live – that is, had to satisfy their basic needs for food, clothing, shelter, and so on. It was these basic needs and nothing more "spiritual" that stimulated the human being to seek within the natural world the objects and means that satisfied those needs.

The relationship between man and nature, understood as a relationship between a human need and the natural object that satisfies it, was seen as the basis for the movement of history. It was a dynamic, dialectical relationship that did not disappear when the primary need had been satisfied; indeed, this satisfaction and the instrument adopted for bringing it about led in turn to new needs and the search for new means of satisfying them.

The mediation between the two poles of need and satisfaction of that need, and therefore between humankind and nature, was effected, according to Marx, by labor. It was through labor – human work – that humanity created the instruments by which to obtain from nature the things that it needed.

Every historical period is characterized by a certain level of development of its *productive forces.* This is a term that denotes the complex of needs and means of production (techniques and technologies, knowledge, individuals, and so on) employed to satisfy those needs. To these forces correspond specific *relations of production,* of labor, that link together the individuals dedicated to the manufacture of the material goods that are necessary for life.

Marx called the ensemble or system comprised of the relations of production and the productive forces the *mode of production.* The mode of production was the true basis of society: it was what determined the organization of society at every level and in every sphere: law, politics, institutions, and so on. It was upon this material foundation (the "structure") that all those phenomena commonly associated with the consciousness or the spirit (the "superstructure") were constructed and developed.

Following is the concise form in which Marx expressed the fundamental concept of historical materialism in the preface to his 1859 work *A Contribution to the Critique of Political Economy:*

> In the social production of their existence, men inevitably enter into definite relations, which are independent of their will, namely relations of production appropriate to a given stage in the development of their material forces of production. The totality of these relations of production constitutes the economic structure of society, the real foundation on which arises a legal and political superstructure and to which correspond definite forms of social consciousness. The mode of production of material life conditions the general process of social, political and intellectual life. It is not the consciousness of men that determines their existence, but their social existence that determines their consciousness.[12]

It was on the basis of these principles that Marx reconstructed the history of human societies from the first tribal groupings to the bourgeois society of his time. For Marx, history was the history of the various modes of production by and through which human beings had produced the material things that were necessary for life. The passage or transition from one mode of production to the next was not linear and continuous, however, but occurred as a rupture in or "break" with the preceding order; this rupture was set off, or triggered, by an internal dialectic. A mode of production entered into crisis when its basic elements – the forces of production and the social relations of production – became reciprocally contradictory. At that point there occurred a *revolutionary* transformation, and a new mode of production emerged. With it, there also emerged a new "culture," a new "consciousness," which supplanted those that had formerly prevailed. Marx says:

12. Marx, *A Contribution to the Critique of Political Economy,* 20. Hereafter cited as *Critique.*

At a certain stage of development, the material productive
forces of society come into conflict with the existing relations
of production, or – this merely expresses the same thing in
legal terms – with the property relations within the framework of which they have operated hitherto. From forms of
development of the productive forces these relations turn into
their fetters. Then begins an era of social revolution. The
changes in the economic foundation lead sooner or later to
the transformation of the whole immense superstructure
(*Critique,* 21).

This was the historical destiny that Marx believed was in
store for a bourgeois society founded upon industrial labor,
the private ownership of the means of production, and the
hegemony of capital. But in comparison with former modes
of production (the medieval, the slave economy of the ancient world, and so on), the capitalist system possesses some
unique characteristics: it is continually forced to revolutionize the forces of production and constantly give them
impetus for growth. Capitalism's field of action spans the
entire globe: it extracts raw materials from the most distant
sites and then takes its finished products into every land,
however isolated that land might be. But in Marx's view, an
irresolvable contradiction between the forces of production
and the social relations of production threatens capitalism;
indeed, the increasingly accentuated social nature of industrial processes of production, Marx believed, was in obvious
conflict with the private ownership of the means of production.

The force that Marx believed was to put an end to the
rule of the capitalist bourgeoisie was the dialectical opposite,
the mirror-negative, of all the characteristics of the bourgeoisie: the proletariat. Here is how Marx expresses this
idea:

In the development of productive forces there comes a stage at which productive forces and means of intercourse are called into existence, which, under the existing relationships, only cause mischief, and which are no longer productive but destructive forces (machinery and money); and connected with this a class is called forth, which has to bear all the burdens of society without enjoying its advantages, which [class], ousted from society, is forced into the most decided antagonism to all other classes; a class which forms the majority of all members of society, and from which emanates the consciousness of the necessity of a fundamental revolution, the communist consciousness.[13]

The disappearance of the bourgeoisie and the victory of the proletariat, however, were themselves determined by the material conditions of the society, not by a purely voluntary revolutionary impulse. In this regard, Marx says: "No social order is ever destroyed before all the productive forces for which it is sufficient have been developed, and new superior relations of production never replace older ones before the material conditions for their existence have matured within the framework of the old society" (*Critique*, 21).

Still, in whatever way it finally came about, the triumph of the proletarian revolution was assured because it was necessarily inscribed within the dynamic of historical evolution. The promise of the revolution was that it would establish a new mode of production – communism – that was more advanced than capitalism. With the abolition of private ownership of property and the socialization of the means of production, communism would bring the relations of production into harmony with the social nature of the forces of production, and thus capitalism's contradictions would be resolved and the forces of production would be led to a new and extraordinary stage of development. For Marx, the cre-

13. Marx and Engels, *The German Ideology*, 68–69.

ation of a communist society would end the process of history or, rather, it would end the prehistory of humanity and usher in a radically new phase of human social existence.

These are, in brief, the central ideas of historical materialism. From the texts we have quoted (those texts generally considered of fundamental importance to an understanding of Marx's thought), what seems to emerge is a conception of history formed around a central core of radical materialism. It should come as no surprise, then, that from the beginning many followers and analysts of Marxism have interpreted it in this way. Indeed, in this view of Marxist thought, nothing stands above the forces of production, from which there derive and upon which there depend both the organization of society and the spiritual manifestations of the human being.

Of course, such a view of society and of history presented many problems. In particular, the relationship between the economic structure and the superstructure (for Marx, those phenomena commonly associated with the consciousness or spirit such as law, politics, philosophy, and religion) was not at all clear. Nor was this merely a "theoretical" issue, since it had a direct bearing on fundamental political and organizational questions relating to the workers' movement. What, for example, was the role of such a superstructural aspect as the "communist" or "revolutionary consciousness," whose bearer, according to Marx, was the proletariat? And how did this "consciousness" act upon the economic structure of society? In practical terms this problem was stated as follows: How and when, in the stage when capitalism falls into its decline, should the proletariat (or rather, its most "conscious" part, the Communist Party) make intentional use of violence? On the basis of Marx's explicit writings, the answer is unclear. On the one hand, Marx granted the proletariat and its organizations a fundamental role in the fall (or toppling) of capitalism while, on the other, in his theory the collapse appears to be the result of intrinsic laws governing the development of capital. If one considers the analysis of the evolution of capitalism as Marx presents it in his 1867 work *Capital (Das Kapital)*, one has the impression that the process that leads to the fall of the bourgeois order is determined by inflexible mechanisms, iron laws that are virtually as quantitative as those of the physical sciences. Marx, in fact, considered his analysis of capitalism to be "scientific" in that it possessed the predictive ability of the exact sciences. In such a rigidly deterministic process, the communist consciousness appears to play only a secondary role.

Following Marx's death in 1883, the debate over the ways the proletariat was to be organized and the ways it was to act in the face of the "inevitable fall" of capitalism became so heated that Engels himself felt obliged to intervene. In his famous letter to Bloch (1890), Engels explained that the materialist conception of history had been misunderstood, that those who saw the forces of production as being absolute and unidirectional determinants of human consciousness and the superstructures of society had twisted and distorted Marx's ideas. It was true that *in the final analysis* the economic structure was the key determinant in the historical process, but it was not the *only* operative factor. Many different aspects of superstructures – the political forms taken by the class struggle, the judicial order of the State, even philosophical and religious beliefs – also exerted their influence on the course of historical events. And while their influence was not *decisive*, it was not to be underestimated, either; it had to be taken into account.

In spite of Engels' clarification, the question of the relationship between structure and superstructure has never ceased to be a source of theoretical debate both inside and outside of Marxist parties. In fact, the question resurfaced dramatically on the eve of World War I when a majority of the German Social Democratic Party voted in favor of Germany's entrance into the war. The German proletariat – the most "conscious" and best organized in Europe – sided with that country's bourgeoisie against the proletariats of France and England, which supported their respective national bourgeoisies in deciding to go to war with Germany. Thus, an element as totally superstructural as national identity had prevailed over the "objective" interests of the various European proletariats, interests that "should have" dictated that the several proletariats unite in combating the oppression they were subjected to by their respective national bourgeoisies.

With regard to the term *dialectical materialism* we should make clear that it was never used by Marx to designate his philosophical formulation; that particular usage became common with Lenin and, in the time of Stalin, as we have noted, came to refer to the official doctrine of the Marxist-Leninist Party in power in the Soviet Union. The concept of dialectical materialism was a theoretical construct formulated almost exclusively by Soviet Marxism on the basis of Engels' reflections on the natural world that he had developed in several works, especially his 1878 *Anti-Dühring* and "The Dialectic of Nature," the latter being an incomplete and fragmentary work to which Engels had intermittently dedicated several years, and which was published posthumously in the Soviet Union in 1925.

Engels, Marx's friend for forty years and his collaborator in writing several works, was fascinated by military strategy and showed a great interest in the sciences. These interests led him to correspond with numerous researchers. In the realm of science, his interest turned toward the formulation of a general philosophy of natural phenomena that would explain the great scientific discoveries of his time (the cell, the conservation of energy, the evolution of species, and so on) and at the same time constitute an objective (that is, "scientific") foundation for Marx's conception of history.

Recognizing the danger inherent in the dichotomy between philosophical and scientific knowledge, Engels criticized the scientific researchers of his time for their single-minded empiricism and their scant mastery of philosophy: they carried out their experimentation in narrow and separate fields and were incapable of framing or grounding their discoveries philosophically. In fact, science in the nineteenth century tended to treat the world, or nature, as a system of fixed and isolatable entities that were to be studied separately and individually, and it explained natural transformations as mechanical interactions between these fixed entities. In Engels' view, such naive "mechanicism" was simply bad philosophy, the remnants of an eighteenth-century world view that prevented an understanding of the continuous flow, the evolutionary unfolding of nature that Darwin had so brilliantly described. For Engels, who was a great admirer of Darwin (1809–1882), the natural world should instead be studied as a system of *relations,* of *dynamic processes,* as the evolutionary development of reciprocally-influencing structures. To explain the complex dynamics of natural phenomena, Engels turned to the laws of dialectics as formulated by Hegel.

Georg Wilhelm Friedrich Hegel (1770–1831) had revolutionized the way of thought that had been traditional since the time of Aristotle by eliminating the two classic principles of logic – identity and non-contradiction – and setting in their place, as the central axis of his new logic, the principle of contradiction. For him, the contradictory character of ideas on reality in no way demonstrated that such ideas were illusory, that there was some unbridgeable chasm between

Reason and Reality. On the contrary – for Hegel, contradiction is an essential property not only of thought but of reality itself.

A concept appears in its fixed identity, totally separate from its contrary, only to an intellectualistic, abstract, and static way of thinking. Hegel's dialectical logic maintains that opposites are not mutually unrelated, but rather that each one is what it is by virtue of its opposition to its contrary; each is defined by being that which the other is not. Any concept understood as positive implies its corresponding negative, its own specific negation: moral good exists only in opposition to its contrary, evil; life is life only in relation to that which constitutes its negation, death; and so on. Thus, a thing is never simply positivity, but always contains within itself its own negativity.

Reason itself has two fundamental tasks: one negative, to dissolve fixed and accepted concepts (by negating or denying them), and another positive, which consists of recognizing that the opposition between contrary concepts may be overcome (negation of the negation) and resolved into a higher unity containing both – the synthesis. That synthesis, in turn, becomes the thesis for a new negation (its antithesis), and the process begins again.

In *Phenomenology of Spirit* (1807) Hegel argued that this dialectical process constituted the path by which the human consciousness had gradually risen from the most naive and "natural" forms to higher and more complex ones – self-consciousness, reason, and spirit. Hegel reconstructed the distinct "figures" of limited, "apparent" knowledge (hence his use of the term *phenomenology*) through which consciousness passed in its evolution. Each "figure" was transformed into its negation, which was followed by a synthesis, a reconciliation of opposites, which in turn became the point of departure for a new stage, for a more complete knowledge that included within itself the preceding stage. The process would conclude when the stage was reached in which consciousness, as "absolute knowledge," reconciled and surpassed the opposition between truth and certainty (what it believes to be truth), between reality and reason.

Engels adopted Hegel's framework of evolution but inverted its terms: that which developed through a dialectical dynamic was not a spiritual principle but matter. For Engels, nature, including living species and humankind, was *matter*, which possessed within itself the motive force of its own dynamics, so that no intervention by a transcendent principle was necessary. Not without reason has dialectical materialism been defined, then, paraphrasing Hegel, as a "phenomenology of the anti-spirit."[14]

This inversion performed on Hegelian dialectics (this "setting right," as Engels smugly called it) corresponds point for point with that inversion carried out by Marx on the Hegelian concept of society and history; but Engels, unlike Marx (whose relations with Hegelian dialectics were ambiguous), *consciously* adopted dialectical logic and even came to claim for it a positive, "scientific" validity. In Engels' view, the laws of thought *were* the laws of the dialectics of nature: the dynamics of knowledge were a "mirror," a reflection, of the dynamics of reality. With this synthesis of idealism and materialism, of Hegel and Darwin, Engels attempted to mend the rift between philosophical and scientific thought and to lay the foundation for the construction of a new and comprehensive science that would overcome the specialization and compartmentalization of the empirical sciences and their exasperatingly analytical and fragmented view of nature and reality.

14. This phrase is from T. W. Adorno.

These ideas were taken up by Lenin, who organized and systematized the diffuse reflections of Engels, giving particular attention to the "mirror" theory that Engels had done little more than outline. But the most salient point is that with Lenin the theory of the evolution of matter takes precedence over Marx's conception of history. Stalin, in turn, was to reaffirm this position and even to give it the force of orthodoxy in his famous 1938 writing *Dialectical and Historical Materialism.*

But dialectical materialism was not easily reconciled with the Marxist conception of history, which it sought to legitimate: for Marx, the basic dialectical relationship was between humanity and nature, from which humanity obtained the objects that served to satisfy its needs. In dialectical materialism, however, this relationship became completely out of balance, because humanity was reduced to an epiphenomenon, a secondary and unnecessary product of the evolution of matter, and the development of human societies, which Marx had attempted to explain from prehistory to the triumph and crisis of the European bourgeoisie, became no more than a brief chapter in the natural history of the world.

Moreover, by affirming the equivalence of the laws of thought and the "scientific" laws that were immanent in nature, Engels' ideas were as "idealistic" as they were "materialistic," so that the distinction between reality and thought tended to disappear, exactly as in the Hegelian philosophy that Engels had claimed to "set right." In fact, if one says that the laws of thought are a reflection, a "copy" of the laws of reality, one could just as well claim that the laws of reality are a reflection of the laws of thought. Paradoxically, dialectical materialism would then turn out to be a restatement of the philosophy of nature enunciated by German romanticism.

And there is yet another problem: the heuristic ability of the new "science" of dialectics – which ought to impart structure and a global perspective to the empirical sciences – was virtually nil. When Engels attempted to apply the laws of dialectics to all fields of knowledge, he was forced into very strained positions, sometimes offering proofs for his theories that were too generic or that were invalidated by later investigations.

The following example should be sufficient to suggest the arbitrariness with which Engels applied the dialectic method in fields such as mathematics, in this case specifically the "negation of the negation" as applied to algebra: "Let us," Engels says, "take any algebraic quantity whatever: for example, a. If this is negated, we get $-a$ (minus a). If we negate that negation, by multiplying $-a$ by $-a$, we get $+a^2$, i.e., the original positive quantity, but at a higher degree, raised to its second power."[15]

Even more deplorable were the dogmatic applications of dialectical materialism in the Soviet Union. One of the best-known cases is that of the biologist T.D. Lysenko, who engaged in open dispute with Western geneticists. Western geneticists maintained the thesis of the invariability of the gene – understood as a determining hereditary factor – down through the generations, whereas for Lysenko, any theory that postulated the fixity of a biological structure was *necessarily* false since it was incompatible with dialectical materialism. Lysenko put his genetic theories into practice in Soviet agriculture, with such disastrous results that within a short time he had disappeared from both the scientific and political scenes.

15. Brief excerpt from *Anti-Dühring* cited in Monod, *Chance and Necessity: An Essay on the Natural Philosophy of Modern Biology*, 39, as an example of what Monod calls "animistic projection" in Engels' scientific thought.

These, in brief summary, are the fundamental ideas of dialectical materialism, a doctrine that acquired increasing importance within the international Marxist movement as the political power of the Soviet Union grew. As we have seen, Engels' writings carried great weight in the formulation of this interpretation of Marxism, but his influence was equally great in the formation of the interpretation of Marxist thought that saw Marxism as a "science" – in the positivistic sense of the word – of society and history.

At this point a clarification is in order. The role played by Engels in the construction of the "scientific" image of Marxism at the end of the nineteenth century is explained not only by the cultural climate of the time and the interest Engels showed in the experimental disciplines, but also by the fact that the works of Marx were known only very partially. At that time, Marx was known principally as the author of *Capital,* a volume on political economy. His only truly philosophical texts were his introductions to the various editions of *Capital* and his famous albeit brief introduction to the 1859 *Contribution to the Critique of Political Economy,* which, as we have seen, contained a summary of the ideas of historical materialism. Most of the texts of the young Marx that would allow one to understand the philosophical and methodological foundations of his thought (his 1844 *Critique of Hegel's "Philosophy of Right,"* the *Economic and Philosophical Manuscripts of 1844,* and *The German Ideology,* written 1845–6) went unpublished until the 1930s, and it was only then, too, that critics first had access to important published texts of his mature years such as his *Grundrisse* and *Theories of Surplus Value.* And as we shall shortly see in more detail, it was above all on the foundation of Marx's early works that the humanist interpretation of Marxism was constructed.

Although the existence of some of the texts that were later to play a key role in the reinterpretation of Marxist thought was then unknown, by the early 1920s the line of interpretation that viewed Marxism as a "science" (whether in the positivistic or the dialectical sense of the word) had begun to come under harsh criticism from eminent theorists outside the Soviet Union. Lukács, Korsch, and later Gramsci (each in his own way) took sharp issue with the view of Marxism as a science and with the contention that its method was congruent with or had to derive from the experimental disciplines. For these writers, Marxism was, on the contrary, fundamentally a critique of bourgeois society and a doctrine of social revolution aimed at liberating human beings from all the alienations to which the capitalist system had condemned them. Lukács, for instance, brought once more to the foreground of Marxist thought the theory of alienation and the fetishism of material goods, clearly stated in *Capital* but virtually ignored by later commentators; indeed, Lukács saw this principle as one of the fundamental aspects of Marx's thought.

For this line of interpretation (which was given the name "Western Marxism"), the true nucleus of Marxist thought, the theoretical center that contained its revolutionary impulse, was dialectics. In this view, dialectics is a theoretical and practical method for understanding human history and human societies, and cannot be extended to or assimilated into a description of the natural world as the empirical sciences understand that world. If it were, then dialectics would necessarily take on the characteristics of those sciences, that is, become a cause-and-effect mechanism, a deterministic connection between events or data. In Western Marxism, in contrast, dialectics postulates the negation of a historically given world, a world divided, alienated, which is to be overcome and reconstituted in its totality through an act of revolution. Thus, Lukács says, dialectics is incompatible with the logic of the empirical sciences, which breaks the world down into separate and disconnected "data," and is therefore the same logic as that of industrial production in capitalism, in which the division of labor becomes an oppressive burden and the worker is transformed into an object, a thing, a "natural fact." One twists and distorts Marx's thought, Lukács argued, when one attempts to adopt the research methods of the empirical sciences or attempts a "scientific" interpretation of dialectics in order to understand human history and human societies.

Gramsci harshly attacked the theories of Engels and his Russian followers on the grounds that they projected onto the human world a determinism that did not exist. Human beings were indeed conditioned by a certain mode of production and by certain superstructures, but precisely because they were human and not simply natural objects they were capable of transforming their historical situations by means of a "raising of consciousness" and revolutionary practice. A crude evolutionism and a naturalistic determinism such as Engels proposed could never explain historical transformations. Gramsci even came to deny that Marxism was a materialism, and attacked the very idea of "objective reality" that forms the basis of the empirical sciences. Belief in "reality," in the objectivity of the world (and here Gramsci harks back directly to Hegel) was but the first stage of human awareness, a stage that corresponded to a naively "natural" consciousness. The word *objective* always meant "historically subjective" for Gramsci, whose view never admitted "mirror" theories of reflection. Essentially, Gramsci saw in Marxism a historicism and a humanism.

The reaction of Soviet Marxism to the ideas of Lukács and Korsch was one of total rejection. The Fifth Congress of the Communist International, held in Moscow in 1924, branded them "revisionists." Meanwhile, the political picture in Europe was changing drastically, and with the rise to power of Italian and German fascisms, the development of Marxism was interrupted in two of the three places where it had known the greatest vitality. In the third, Russia, Marxism was transformed under Stalin into a sort of state religion that legitimized the power structure of the bureaucratic elite of the Soviet Communist Party and, in consequence, the Communist parties operating in capitalist countries.

But the reappearance of the texts of Marx's youth, particularly his *Economic and Philosophic Manuscripts of 1844,* which were rediscovered only by accident in Paris, revealed beyond any doubt the strong current of humanism in Marx and attested to a critical, libertarian attitude on his part. Taken together, these two tendencies constituted a radical and total discrediting of the bureaucracies of the Communist Parties then in power. The attitude of these bureaucracies toward the works of the young Marx was to dismiss them simply as ground-laying works, works that were still "immature," preparatory exercises for the philosophy that would fully manifest itself only later on. The libertarian spirit of these works was branded as "ideology" by the bureaucracies, which in Marxist terminology signified any representation that covered the true, "scientific" reality of facts and things with a veneer of false and illusory images. It was, of course, precisely *against* such ideologies, *against* such superstructures (whether of law, politics, philosophy, religion, and so forth) that Marx had put forth his materialist conception of history.

For Marx, the production of ideologies presupposed the prior existence of a fundamental social division of labor – that is, a division between manual work and intellectual work. It was by virtue of this dichotomy that there arose groups of "professional intellectuals" who operated in specialized fields, giving rise to more or less complex institutional structures. The function of these ideology-producing intellectual fringes was mainly to paper over and justify the division of classes within the society, to conceal and justify the exploitation of manual work. Starting with this fundamental lie, these intellectual fringes constructed an inverted and idealized image of social and historical reality.

Grotesquely, and without the slightest capacity for self-criticism, the intellectuals linked to the Party bureaucracies did not hesitate to accuse the young Marx himself of "ideology" or to set against the young Marx the mature, "scientific" Marx of the later works. The juvenilia themselves were even censored, and entire passages of some of the mature texts were blacked out.[16]

In the years after World War II, however – and here we take up the thread of our initial argument – it began to be clear that the Russian model had produced with Stalinism a monstrous dictatorship that trampled upon fundamental human rights and the most elementary forms of personal liberty. It was within this cultural climate that an interest in recovering and giving due value to the humanist aspects of Marx's thought began to arise within those philosophical circles of Marxism that were unaligned with Party bureaucracies. And so it was that the line of interpretation called "Marxist humanism" began to develop, a line of thought opposed to "dialectical materialism" and, more generally, to all those interpretations that portrayed Marxism as a "science" of economics and history.

Let us look, then, at Marx's conception of the human being and at how his younger works presented humanism.

16. For an analysis of distortions in Soviet Marxism see Marcuse, *Soviet Marxism*.

In the *Manuscripts of 1844*, the twenty-six-year-old Marx had criticized Hegelian idealism (according to which the human being was only a spiritual being, a self-consciousness) and sketched the broad outlines of his own anthropology. For Marx, man is above all a natural, material being. The various definitions that Marx gives in these manuscripts forcefully underscore this aspect of the human being. Man is a "*corporeal*, living, real, sensuous, objective being full of natural vigor."[17] In addition, man, as a:

> natural being and as a living natural being ... is on the one hand endowed with *natural powers of life* – he is an *active* natural being. These forces exist in him as tendencies and abilities – as *instincts*. On the other hand, as a natural, corporeal, sensuous, objective being he is a *suffering*, conditioned and limited creature, like animals and plants. That is to say, the *objects* of his instincts exist outside him, as *objects* independent of him; yet these objects are *objects* that he *needs* – essential *objects*, indispensable to the manifestation and confirmation of his essential powers (*1844 Mss*, 181).

We see, then, that man lives within the horizon of the natural world, from which he, like all other sentient beings, receives impressions and conditionings, and in which he is able to find the things that satisfy his needs, things toward which his internal impulses (understood as natural forces) draw him. And the world that surrounds him is a real and objective world. This concept of man and the world clearly derives from Feuerbach, who, disagreeing with Hegel, considered both man and the world to be objective natural entities.

Even so, the *Manuscripts of 1844* clearly show how far Marx had strayed from the rigorous naturalism of Feuerbach. For Marx, "man is not merely a natural being: he is a

---

17. Marx, *Economic and Philosophic Manuscripts of 1844*, 181. Hereafter cited as *1844 Mss*.

human natural being. That is to say, he is a being for himself. Therefore he is a *species being,* and has to confirm and manifest himself as such both in his being and in his knowing. Therefore, *human* objects are not natural objects as they immediately present themselves" (*1844 Mss,*182). "But *nature,* too, taken abstractly, for itself – nature fixed in isolation from man – is *nothing* for man" (*1844 Mss,*191).

In other words, man has certain specific characteristics that distinguish him from other natural beings: he is a consciousness (a being-for-himself) that manifests itself as knowing. He is not simply nature. Natural objects, in turn, while real, cannot be conceived in and of themselves, independent of the activities of human beings. The relation between the human being and nature does not therefore reside in a faithful "reflection" of the reality of nature in the human consciousness (as Engels and Lenin would later maintain) or in a simple conditioning of the human being by nature; it is, rather, a relationship that is eminently active, practical. Through conscious activity (labor) the human being "objectifies" itself into the natural world, drawing that world ever nearer, making it ever more human. What was once simple nature is now transformed into a human product. Therefore, if man is a natural being, nature in turn is *humanized nature,* that is, consciously transformed by man himself. Marx says that "the *entire so-called history of the world* is nothing but the creation of man through human labor, nothing but the emergence of nature for man" (*1844 Mss,*145). "It is just in his work upon the objective world, therefore, that man first really proves himself to be a *species being.* This production is his active species life. Through and because of this production, nature appears as *his* work and his reality" (*1844 Mss,* 114).

For Marx, the uniqueness of the human being, the fundamental attribute that makes a human being part of a particular natural species, the *human* species, lies in the human ability to transform nature by work. Humankind is fundamentally *homo laborans,* "working man." Several aspects of this idea were derived by Marx from Hegel, who had maintained in his *Phenomenology of Spirit* (though from a different standpoint) that all historical, social, cultural, and even natural reality is the product of the activity of human beings, an "objectivization" of human consciousness. For Hegel, too, labor – which simultaneously transforms both nature and the human being itself – constitutes the life and the consciousness of the human species.

The other fundamental aspect of Marx's anthropology (closely linked to the foregoing) is found in his declaration that man is, in essence, social: "[M]an is in the most literal sense of the word a *zoon politikon,* not only a social animal, but an animal which can develop into an individual only in society."[18] "[T]he human essence is no abstraction inherent in each single individual. In its reality it is the ensemble of the social relations."[19]

The essence of humanity, then, resides not in some characteristic that can be located within each individual, in the individual's "consciousness," but on the contrary can only be found, in a manner of speaking, outside the person – in society, in the complex of social relations that the individual establishes with others. Working together to transform nature, people construct a sort of "collective being" that is social and communitarian. And it is only there that the essence of humanity is fully manifested:

> *Exchange,* both of human activity within production itself and of *human products* against one another, is equivalent

18. Cited in "Editor's Introduction," Marx, *Critique of Hegel's "Philosophy of Right,"* xliii.
19. Marx, *Reader in Marxist Philosophy,* "Theses on Feuerbach," thesis VI, 317. Also in Marx and Engels, *Collected Works,* 5:7.

to *species-activity* and species-spirit, the real, conscious and true mode of existence of which is *social* activity and *social* enjoyment. Since *human* nature is the *true community* of men, by manifesting their nature men *create,* produce, the *human community,* the social entity, which is no abstract universal power opposed to the single individual, but is the essential nature of each individual, his own activity, his own life, his own spirit, his own wealth.[20]

Man is transformed from a natural being into a truly *human* being only in society. And only in society are we able to understand and carry out the task that has been assigned to the species: the humanization of nature:

The *human* essence of nature first exists only for *social* man; for only here does nature exist for him as a *bond* with *man* – as his existence for the other and the other's existence for him – as the life-element of human reality. Only here does nature exist as the *foundation* of his own *human* existence. Only here has what is to him his *natural* existence become his *human* existence, and nature become man for him. Thus *society* is the unity of being of man with nature – the true resurrection of nature – the naturalism of man and the humanism of nature both brought to fulfillment (*1844 Mss,* 137).

From this conception there derive two consequences, both of great importance. First of all, that the human being has no fixed "essence." Since the human essence is the whole of social relations, it is necessarily historical and dynamic, changing depending upon the organization of social production and the process of humanization of nature. Thus, the human being does not possess an essence that can be assimilated into an abstract, static concept, that can be defined in any permanent way.

20. Marx, "Comments on James Mill" in Marx and Engels, *Collected Works* 3:216–17. Hereafter cited as "Comments on Mill."

The second consequence is that the natural sociability of the human being cannot manifest itself in its positive aspect so long as labor and production are organized in a noncommunitarian way, without solidarity. So long as such conditions prevail, human sociability will be manifested as "estrangement," "alienation," the distancing or isolation of the individual from him- or herself, from society, from the species, and from nature. These are the words with which Marx expresses this fundamental concept:

> [A]s long as man does not recognise himself as man, and therefore has not organised the world in a human way, this *community* appears in the form of *estrangement,* because its *subject,* man, is a being estranged from himself. Men, not as an abstraction, but as real, living, particular individuals, *are* this entity. Hence, *as* they are, so is this entity itself. To say that *man* is estranged from himself, therefore, is the same thing as saying that the *society* of this estranged man is a caricature of his *real community,* of his true species-life, that his activity therefore appears to him as a torment, his own creation as an alien power, his wealth as poverty, the *essential bond* linking him with other men as an unessential bond, and separation from his fellow men, on the other hand, as his true mode of existence ("Comments on Mill," 217).

Marx discovered the origin of alienation or estrangement in the private ownership of property, which in capitalist society dominates all aspects of individual and collective life. In Marx's view, capitalism reduced the individual human being to the labor that he or she was able to perform, to the merchandise that he or she produced. Thus, the individual had been transformed into merchandise, a *thing.* In opposition to the individual human being there had arisen, like some sort of Golem, an "alien social power" that was nothing more than the collective being that through their essence human beings always construct, but which, because it was the result of non-communitarian production, dominated, like some independent force, the very people who had given it life.

This is the way Marx describes this "war of all against all" in capitalist society:

> [E]very person speculates on creating a *new* need in another, so as to drive him to a fresh sacrifice, to place him in a new dependence.... Each tries to establish over the other an *alien power,* so as thereby to find satisfaction of his own selfish need. The increase in the quantity of objects is accompanied by an extension of the realm of the alien powers to which man is subjected, and every new product represents a new *possibility* of mutual swindling and mutual plundering. Man becomes ever poorer as man, his need for *money* becomes ever greater if he wants to overpower hostile being. The power of his *money* declines so to say in inverse proportion to the increase in the volume of production: that is, his neediness grows as the *power* of money increases (*1844 Mss,* 147).

But alienation, estrangement, is not limited to the relationship between individuals; it produces a schism, a rupture inside the individual as well, altering even the structure of the individual's perceptions. "Private property has made us so stupid and one-sided that an object is only *ours* when we have it – when it exists for us as capital, or when it is directly possessed, eaten, drunk, worn, inhabited, etc., – in short, when it is *used* by us.... *All* these physical and mental senses have therefore – the sheer estrangement of *all* these senses – the sense of *having*" (*1844 Mss,* 139). "[T]he *senses* of the social man are *other* senses than those of the non-social man" (*1844 Mss,* 141).

For Marx, doing away with alienation, ending it, is possible only by suppressing its cause – private property. Once that which had negated the individual's and the species' natural sociability was itself negated, that natural sociability would again reassert itself in its fullest and most positive manifestation. With this second inversion, the inverted world would once again be turned right side up. The humanity of the human being would be reestablished and the internal rupture would be healed, as would the individual's rupture with society, the species, and nature:

> The transcendence of private property is therefore the complete *emancipation* of all human senses and qualities, but it is this emancipation precisely because these senses and attributes have become, subjectively and objectively, *human.* The eye has become a *human* eye, just as its *object* has become a social, *human* object – an object made by man for man (*1844 Mss,* 139).

And now let us examine the most complete definition of humanist communism given by Marx:

> Communism [is defined] as the *positive* transcendence of *private property* [understood] as *human self-estrangement,* and therefore as the real *appropriation of the human* essence by and for man; communism [is defined] therefore as the complete return of man to himself as a *social* (i.e., human) being – a return become conscious, and accomplished within the entire wealth of previous development. This communism, as fully developed naturalism, equals humanism, and as fully developed humanism equals naturalism (*1844 Mss,* 135).

But for Marx, this basic theoretical understanding was not sufficient in and of itself; it had to be enacted, put into practice. Philosophy *per se* was no longer enough; it was no longer valid as a mode of existence. One could not content oneself with interpreting the world; it had to be transformed. Philosophy had to commit itself to action, had to orient and guide the transformation of the world, had to become prax-is. Without praxis, philosophy was nothing.[21]

With Marx, then, philosophy became fundamentally ac-tion (labor) and the philosopher a revolutionary. But the very human activity that would negate and transform the in-human conditions of the world would not be possible if the evolution of history were the result of a rigid determinism (as both ancient and modern materialists maintained) or the cleverness of universal Reason, for which the human being served merely as the naive stuff of history (as maintained by Hegel). Marx strongly criticized both of these positions. For him, determinism was not sufficient. The dynamics of history were born out of the union of natural and historical condi-tioning and the free human activity that attempts to modify that conditioning.[22]

This philosophical concept cannot be facilely defined as materialism in the traditional sense. Marx himself in clarify-ing this said at the beginning of the outline of his anthropol-ogy in the *Manuscripts of 1844* that here "we see how consistent naturalism or humanism distinguishes itself [from

21. "Social life is essentially *practical*. All mysteries which mislead theory into mysticism find their rational solution in human practice and in the comprehension of this practice." Similarly, the "philosophers have only *interpreted* the world in various ways; the point, however, is to *change* it." (Marx, *Reader in Marxist Philosophy*, "Theses on Feuerbach," theses VIII and XI; 8).

22. "The materialist doctrine that men are products of circumstances and upbringing, and that, therefore, changed men are products of other circumstances and changed upbringing, forgets that it is men who change circumstances and that the educator himself needs educating. Hence, this doctrine necessarily arrives at dividing society into two parts, of which one is superior to society (in Robert Owen, for exam-ple). The coincidence of the changing of circumstances and of human activity can be conceived and rationally understood only as *revolution-izing practice*." (Marx, *Reader*, "Theses on Feuerbach," thesis III, 316–17).

both] idealism and materialism, constituting at the same time the unifying truth of both" (*1844 Mss,* 181). The concept that emerges from the younger works seems to be, as Marx himself affirmed, a naturalism that coincides with a humanism, in the sense that if the human being is a natural being, nature is always *humanized* nature, that is, transformed by the social labor of humanity.

Marxist humanism is based essentially on the ideas we have cited above. It should come as no surprise, then, that some exponents of this line of interpretation strongly argue that it is not correct to consider Marxism to be a materialism, and in fact claim that the best definition of Marxism is precisely as a "humanism." These are the words of Rodolfo Mondolfo (1877–1976), the first interpreter of Marx to maintain this thesis:

> In reality, if we examine historical materialism without prejudice, just as it is given us in Marx's and Engels' texts, we have to recognize that it is not a materialism but rather a true humanism, [and] that it places the idea of man at the center of every consideration, every discussion. It is a realistic humanism (*realer Humanismus*), as its own creators called it, which wishes to consider man in his effective and concrete reality, to comprehend his existence in history, and to comprehend history as a reality produced by man through activity, labor, social action, down through the centuries in which there gradually occurs the formation and transformation of the environment in which man lives, and in which man himself gradually develops, as simultaneously cause and effect of all historical evolution. In this sense, we find that historical materialism cannot be confused with a materialist philosophy.[23]

But the humanist interpretation of Marx's thought found vehement opposition among the proponents of a "scientific"

23. Mondolfo, *Umanismo di Marx,* 312–13.

Marxism. One of the best known of these proponents, the French thinker Louis Althusser, has written that "precisely in the couple 'humanism-socialism' there is a striking theoretical unevenness: in the framework of the Marxist conception, the concept 'socialism' is indeed a scientific concept, but the concept 'humanism' is no more than an *ideological* one."[24]

Though acknowledging that the young Marx went through a humanist phase, Althusser argues that:

> [I]n 1845, Marx broke radically with every theory that based history and politics on an essence of man. This unique rupture contained three indissociable elements.
> (1) The formation of a theory of history and politics based on radically new concepts: the concepts of social formation, productive forces, relations of production, superstructure, ideologies, determination in the last instance by the economy, specific determination of the other levels, etc.
> (2) A radical critique of the *theoretical* pretensions of every philosophical humanism.
> (3) The definition of humanism as an *ideology* (*For Marx*, 227).

Althusser maintains that there was a moment of rupture and change in Marx's production, a sort of "conversion" from a humanist phase to a strictly scientific one. With the formulation of the key concepts of historical materialism and the critique of philosophical humanisms, Marx had moved beyond any "ideological" conception, any conception not grounded in a scientific analysis of the economic phenomena that are the basis of historical evolution.

This is the theory of the "two Marxes" (the still-ideological young Marx and the truly scientific mature Marx), which was in substantial alignment with the "official" theory of the

24. Althusser, *For Marx*, 223. Hereafter cited as *For Marx*.

Soviet Marxist-Leninist Party. The consequences Althusser derives from this position are the following:

> [A]ny thought that appeals to Marx for any kind of restoration of a theoretical anthropology or humanism is no more than ashes, *theoretically*. But in practice it could pile up a monument of pre-Marxist ideology that would weigh down on real history and threaten to lead it into blind alleys (*For Marx*, 229–30):

> When (eventually) a Marxist policy of humanist ideology, that is, a political attitude to humanism, is achieved – a policy which may be either a rejection or a critique, or a use, or a support, or a development, or a humanist renewal of contemporary forms of ideology in the *ethico-political* domain – this policy will only have been possible on the absolute condition that it is based on Marxist philosophy, and a precondition for this is theoretical *anti-humanism* (*For Marx*, 231).

Thus Althusser, portraying himself as the interpreter of the original thought of Marx, staunchly denies that Marxism is a humanism; on the contrary, it is Althusser's contention that Marxism, as a "science" of society and history, a historical materialism, is *necessarily* an anti-humanism. According to this point of view, a tactical political relationship between Marxism and various types of humanism may occur – that is, according to circumstances, the politics of the moment may call for rejection, support, or some other position with respect to a given type of humanism – but it must always be clear that Marxism and humanism are antithetical.

It is plain from what we have seen thus far just how wide a divergence of opinion there is even among Marxist interpreters themselves regarding the general significance and meaning of Marx's work. And in recent years, the idea that Marx's work might be considered a humanism has come to divide the Marxist camp into two irreconcilable factions. It is true, of course, that in the history of philosophy markedly different interpretations of a single doctrine are not unusual; one has only to think of the variety of interpretations given Aristotelian thought by the ancient and medieval worlds as well as our own. But in general, new interpretations of a doctrine emerge when that doctrine begins to operate in a historical and cultural context different from that in which it originated. The singular thing about Marxism is that two such opposed interpretations should appear almost simultaneously in the very cultural ambit in which the philosophy came into being. As we have seen, some in the Germanic cultural world viewed Marxism as an essentially *scientific* materialist theory of society based on the study of deterministic cause-effect relationships and therefore (*qua* science) lacking value judgments, while during that identical time period others of the same cultural sphere saw it as a critique of alienated bourgeois society – a critique that necessarily presupposed a comparison with a different, non-bourgeois system of values considered to be "superior."

In the first interpretation, the theory of alienation or dialectics itself is relegated to the margins of Marx's work. In the second interpretation, it is the "scientific" aspects that are set aside as being outmoded and superseded.

But if one looks more closely at this phenomenon, this interpretative dualism can be seen to derive from an underlying ambiguity in the work of Marx itself.[25] As we have noted, Marx combined positivism with idealism, the realm of facts and causation with the realm of goals and values. He attempted to investigate the mechanisms, the causal nexuses that were at work in economic and social formations, producing transformations there. He sought to study human society in the way a researcher coldly plumbs a natural phe-

25. See Kelsen, *The Political Theory of Bolshevism* and *Sozialismus und Staat*. See also Colletti, "Marxismo" in *Enciclopedia del Novecento*, vol. IV.

nomenon, describing its characteristics and its laws precisely and with detachment. But if this attitude is to be coherent, it cannot admit value judgments of economic and social formations on the basis of an ethical ideal. That is, for example, a study of the evolutionary relationships between various species of primates or insects subject to the pressure of their environment cannot entail a moral judgment of those same phenomena.

At the same time Marx was the most impassioned philosopher of his time in denouncing the alienation and reification of the human being (the reduction of the individual to an object, a thing), the dehumanization of the individual in a world turned upside down. His indignation at the exploitation of workers in the industrial age, their poverty and miserable lives, his contempt for the hypocrisy of the bourgeois class and its ideologies, his call to conscious praxis for the transformation of an inhuman and inhumane social reality have constituted one of the harshest moral critiques of capitalist society. In truth, his entire philosophical thought is permeated with an eschatological promise, a yearning toward the ideal. For Marx, throughout the long path of history the human being has been a creature mutilated, bereft of its true essence – labor, undertaken in common cause with other men and women to humanize nature – for the human being is ruler and god, the center of nature. But this history of blood and tears, alienation and subjugation that is the history of humanity was one day to come to an end – the end of History. The ideal society – communism – would one day heal all wounds, reconcile human beings with themselves, with others, and with nature.

It is clear that neither this humanism nor this eschatology (the latter clearly derived from Hegel) is easy to reconcile with the goal of describing economic and social phenomena scientifically, because the humanism and the eschatology are based on goals and value judgments, which Marx himself called "ideologies."

If this analysis is correct, it is possible to say in summary that Marx viewed the human being as a natural entity basically like any other, while at the same time placing the human being, as the world's supreme value, at the center of nature and history. Marx constantly – and sometimes incoherently – oscillated between these two opposing concepts of the human being. In his effort to reconcile them he tried to demonstrate that history, though based on rigid laws of necessity, did progress toward an ultimate end: human liberty. If these two conceptions of humankind are seen as mutually exclusive, then Marxist doctrine can be interpreted in two opposing ways: as a materialism or as a humanism. Understood as a materialism, Marxist doctrine is then itself subject to the very critique Marx leveled against capitalist bourgeois society: that in it the human being is reduced to an object, a thing. Indeed, as Sartre wrote in his polemic against Marxism taken as materialism: "The effect of all materialism is to treat all men, including the one philosophizing, as objects, that is, as an ensemble of determined reactions in no way distinguished from the ensemble of qualities and phenomena which constitute a table or a chair or a stone."[26]

If, on the other hand, Marxism is understood as a humanism, then it can no longer portray itself as a fact-based, law-based science of society and history but is able to play only the role of an interpretation.

---

26. Sartre, *Existentialism*, 43–44. Hereafter cited as *Existentialism*.

2. Christian Humanism

THE REINTERPRETATION of Christianity as a humanism developed in the first half of this century as part of a vast and wide-ranging process, which began in the nineteenth century and continues even today, of revising Christian doctrines to adapt them to the modern world – a world toward which the Catholic Church has held since the Counter Reformation a position of clear rejection if not outright condemnation.

Throughout the Middle Ages the Catholic Church had been the sole repository of the Christian vision in the West. But during the Renaissance, the Church began to feel its spiritual authority increasingly eroded in a cascade of epochal events: the culture of humanism turned upside down the image that medieval Christianity had constructed of humankind, nature, and history; the Protestant Reformation had divided the Christians of Europe; in the seventeenth and especially the eighteenth centuries, the influence of the rationalist *philosophes* and their heirs was felt increasingly in every sphere of intellectual life. All these events had opened the doors to a questioning that extended even to the essence of Christianity itself. In the nineteenth century, religion was further relegated to a marginal position when socialist and liberal ideologies of a generally "scientific" character, which developed more or less in parallel with the expansion of the Industrial Revolution, began to occupy religion's traditional role as the model for the organization of society and the guide for defining its goals and ideals. Finally, in the twentieth century, the swift spread of atheism, which quickly became a mass phenomenon, threatened the very survival of the Church as an institution.

To prevent itself from being swept away, the Church felt increasingly obliged to abandon the view of the world it had inherited from the Middle Ages – and its defense of the social order that followed from such a view. The ensuing process of opening and modernization was hardly linear or easy for the Church, however; it was accompanied by profound internal resistances, changes of direction, and rethinkings.

In the course of the Church's tortuous rapprochement with the modern world, the 1891 encyclical *Rerum Novarum* of Pope Leo XIII (r. 1878–1903) marked an important turning-point. With this encyclical, the Church adopted a social doctrine that could be set against liberalism and socialism. Objecting strongly to socialism, the encyclical reaffirmed the right to private property, though it softened that position with an appeal for solidarity between classes (in the name of the common good) and for reciprocal responsibility between the individual and the community. Against economic liberalism and its *laissez-faire* attitude in matters of the economy, the Church urged the State and the stronger classes to succor the weaker social spheres.

In the aftermath of the tragedy of World War I, in the general climate of disillusionment with the idea of progress that had been held out by socialism and liberalism, the Church went on a determined counterattack, and did so on both the political front, where it authorized the formation of mass-scale Christian Democratic or Christian Socialist parties, and on the doctrinal front, where it presented itself as the bearer of a vision, a faith, and a moral system able to answer to the most profound needs of the modern person.

It was out of this attempt to redefine and reintroduce Christian values (appropriately updated for the modern world) that "Christian Humanism" emerged, a current whose first important proponent is often considered to be the French thinker Jacques Maritain (1882–1973).

Maritain was first a follower of Henri Bergson and then espoused the ideas of revolutionary socialism. Dissatisfied with both philosophies, in 1906 he converted to Catholicism. He was one of the most notable exponents of what was called "neo-Thomism" – that current of modern Catholic thought that could be traced directly back to Saint Thomas Aquinas and through him to Aristotle, whose philosophy Aquinas had attempted to reconcile with Christian dogmas. At this point we should recall that previously, in the late nineteenth century, another encyclical of Pope Leo XIII, the *Æterni Patris* (1879), had declared the thought of Saint Thomas Aquinas to be the theology best suited to the Christian world view.

Maritain, whose position was radically opposed to the general tendency of modern thought, took a great leap backward, as it were, past the Renaissance, to reconnect with the philosophical thought of the Middle Ages. This was necessary, he believed, because it was within the humanism of the Renaissance that he identified the seeds that had grown into the crisis, indeed the breakdown, of modern society – a crisis of which Nazism and Stalinism were the most terrible expressions. Maritain did not of course explicitly propose to reestablish the values of the Middle Ages and the Christian world view associated with that time; his objective was to reestablish, after all the difficulties experienced in the Middle Ages, the continuation of Christianity's historical evolution, which, in Maritain's view, had been interrupted and blocked by modern secular and lay thought.

In his 1936 book *Integral Humanism: Temporal and Spiritual Problems of a New Christendom*, Maritain examines the evolution of modern thought from the crisis of medieval Christianity to the bourgeois individualism of the nineteenth century and the totalitarianism of the twentieth. In this evolution he sees the tragedy of "anthropocentric humanism" (as he calls it), which has taken shape since the Renaissance. This humanism, which has led to a progressive de-Christianization of the West, is, according to Maritain, a metaphysics of "freedom without grace." With the Renaissance, humanity began to see its own destiny and its own freedom as no longer linked to the workings of grace – that is, to God's plan; freedom came to be seen as a privilege that the individual might aspire to achieve by his or her own efforts. Maritain put it this way:

> To [man] alone it belongs henceforth to make his destiny, to himself alone it belongs to intervene like a god, by a dominating knowledge which absorbs within it and surmounts all necessity, in the conduct of his own life and in the functioning of the great machine of the universe delivered over to geometric determinism.[27]

Thus, modern man, as offspring of and heir to the Renaissance, bears within himself the sin of pride. He has wished to dispense with God and to construct for himself a scientific knowledge of nature, a nature that from the time of Descartes onward has been conceived of as a great machine to be studied *more geometrico,* by the laws of geometry. But such a conception of nature can lead only to a rupture between the human being and the world, to a mechanistic determinism that obliterates the human being. In fact, as Reason replaces God and scientific knowledge spreads, the internal crisis of the human being grows ever more profound.

These are the stages in the progressive decay of modern man, who, like Prometheus, rebels against God and, like Faust, is willing to do anything to penetrate the secrets of nature:

27. Maritain, *Integral Humanism,* 21. Hereafter cited as *Integral.*

As regards man, one can note that in the beginnings of the modern age, with Descartes first and then with Rousseau and Kant, rationalism had raised up a proud and splendid image of the *personality* of man, inviolable, jealous of his immanence and his autonomy and, last of all, good in essence. It was in the very name of the rights and autonomy of this personality that the rationalist polemic had condemned any intervention from the outside into this perfect and sacred universe, whether such intervention would come from revelation and grace, from a tradition of human wisdom, from the authority of a law of which man is not the author, from a Sovereign Good which solicits his will, or finally, from an objective reality which would measure and rule his intelligence (*Integral,* 28).

But this rationalist pride, this arrogance, which first eliminated all traditional and transcendent values and then, with idealism, absorbed into itself even objective reality, bore within it the seeds of its own destruction. First Darwin and then Freud dealt mortal blows to the optimistic vision of perpetual progress of anthropocentric humanism. With Darwin (1809–1882), humanity discovered that no biological disjuncture exists between itself and the ape. Even more, no real *metaphysical* discontinuity exists between humanity and the ape – that is, there is no radical difference of essence, no true qualitative leap. With Freud (1856–1939), humankind discovered that its deepest motivations are actually dictated by "a radically sexual libido and an instinct for death" (*Integral,* 29). "*Acheronta movebo* [I will move Hell]" Freud himself says, "and all the well-regulated dignity of our personal conscience appears as a deceitful mask" (*Integral,* 29). With this pronouncement, the arrogance of Reason was swallowed in the quicksand of the instincts.

At the end of this destructive dialectical process, Maritain concluded, the doors had been opened to the modern totalitarianisms of fascism and Stalinism:

> After all the dissociations and dualisms in the age of anthropocentric humanism ... we are now witnessing a dispersion, a final decomposition. This does not prevent man from claiming sovereignty more than ever. But this claim is no longer made for the individual person, for he no longer knows where to find himself, he sees himself only as torn apart from society and fragmentized. Individual man is ripe for abdication ... in favor of collective man, in favor of that great historic image of humanity which for Hegel, who gave us the theology of it, consisted in the State with its perfect juridic structure, and which for Marx will consist in Communist society with its immanent dynamism (*Integral,* 30).

Against an anthropocentric humanism that he describes in this way Maritain sets Christian humanism, which he defines as "integral" or "theocentric." He says:

> We are thus led to distinguish two kinds of humanism: a theocentric or truly Christian humanism; and an anthropocentric humanism, for which the spirit of the Renaissance and that of the Reformation are primarily responsible....
>
> The first kind of humanism recognizes that God is the center of man; it implies the Christian conception of man, sinner and redeemed, and the Christian conception of grace and freedom.... The second kind ... believes that man himself is the center of man, and therefore of all things. It implies a naturalistic conception of man and of freedom.... [O]ne understands [why] anthropocentric humanism merits the name of inhuman humanism, and that its dialectic must be regarded as the tragedy of humanism (*Integral,* 27–28).

The foundation on which theocentric humanism is built is a conception of man:

...as an animal endowed with reason, whose supreme dignity is in the intellect; and man as a free individual in personal relation with God, whose supreme righteousness consists in voluntarily obeying the law of God; and man as a sinful and wounded creature called to divine life and to the freedom of grace, whose supreme perfection consists of love.[28]

Here we can see that Maritain's conception of man is the classical Aristotelian idea of man as a rational animal, interpreted in a Christian context by Saint Thomas Aquinas. Man is neither pure nature nor pure reason; his essence is defined by his relation to God and God's grace. Man understood in this way is a "person."[29]

Within the human person Maritain distinguishes two types of aspirations, the "connatural" and the "transnatural." Through the first, man tends to realize certain specific qualities that make him a particular individual. Man has a right to see his connatural aspirations come to fruition, but their fruition does not leave him fulfilled or completely satisfied, because transnatural aspirations, which spur him to surmount the limits of his human condition, also exist within him. These transnatural aspirations derive from a transcendent element in man and "have no *right* to be satisfied. If they are, somehow, it will come about through divine Grace [emphasis added]."[30]

To theocentric humanism understood in this way Maritain entrusts the task of constructing a "new Christianity" that will be able to return modern secular society to the

28. Maritain, *Education at the Crossroads,* 7.
29. This term has a long history; the original Latin meaning of the word is "mask," and in this sense "role." In late Stoicism it began to be used to refer to the human individual with a role in the world assigned by Fate. The use of the term to indicate the subject of rights – in distinction to, for example, the slave – comes from Roman jurisprudence.
30. Maritain, *De Bergson à Thomas d'Aquin,* 186–88.

values and spirit of the Gospel. But this renewed Christian civilization must not repeat the errors of the Middle Ages, especially in the attempt to subject political power to religious power. It should instead strive to integrate the two types of human aspirations and thereby harmonize profane activities with the spiritual aspect of existence.

Maritain's Christian interpretation of humanism was enthusiastically embraced by certain segments of the Church as well as various lay groups. It inspired a number of Catholic movements committed to social action and political life and so turned out to be an effective ideological weapon, especially against Marxism. But this interpretation also received witheringly effective criticism from nonconfessional philosophical spheres. The first difficulty to be pointed out was that the rationalist tendency that had appeared in post-Renaissance philosophy and that Maritain had denounced in Descartes, Kant, and Hegel could in fact be traced to the thought of Saint Thomas Aquinas himself. This tendency, which had led to the crisis and eventual defeat of Reason, was not the product of Renaissance humanism but of Thomism and late Scholasticism; the rationalism of the Cartesian philosophy that lies at the foundation of modern thought is much more closely connected to Saint Thomas than to the Neoplatonism and mystical Hermeticism of the Renaissance. The roots of modern philosophy's "arrogance of Reason" should be sought instead, these critics pointed out, in the attempt by Thomism to construct an intellectualist and abstract form of theology. In their view, Maritain had carried out a massive work of mystification and camouflage, almost a game of philosophical prestidigitation, attributing to the Renaissance the historical responsibility that in actuality belonged to late-medieval thought.

In the second place, the crisis of values, the existential vacuum that had appeared in European thought with Darwin, Nietzsche, and Freud, was not, argued Maritain's critics, a consequence of Renaissance humanism, but on the contrary derived from the persistence of medieval Christian ideas within modern society. The tendency toward dualism and dogmatism, the sense of guilt, the rejection of the body and sexuality, the devaluation of women, the fear of death and Hell – all these things are the remnants of medieval Christianity, which long after the Renaissance continue to exert a powerful influence on Western thought. In fact, critics argued, it was these tendencies, strongly reaffirmed in the Reformation and the Counter Reformation, that have determined the sociocultural environment in which modern thought took shape. The schizophrenia of the present-day world (a schizophrenia upon which Maritain insisted) derived, these critics argued, from the simultaneous coexistence of both *human* and *antihuman* values. The "destructive dialectic" of the West could best be explained, then, as a painful and frustrated attempt to free itself from the conflict between these warring values.

3. Existentialist Humanism

IMMEDIATELY after World War II the cultural landscape of France was dominated by the figure of Jean-Paul Sartre (1905–1980) and the current of thought known as "existentialism," which his philosophical and fictional works, along with his own *engagement* or politico-cultural commitment, helped to spread throughout not only France but the entire Western world.

Sartre's strongest philosophical influence came from the school of phenomenology through his contact with the thought of Husserl and Heidegger during his studies in Germany in 1933–34. In phenomenology and its investigative method, which emphasize the intentionality of the consciousness, Sartre found the vehicle for moving beyond the academic French philosophy of his day, which was strongly tinged with spiritualism and idealism and which Sartre completely rejected.

Sartre's search began in the field of psychology; indeed, his ambition as a young man was to revolutionize the foundations of that discipline. Sartre was deeply dissatisfied with modern psychology and its positivistic tendencies, its insistence upon treating psychic phenomena as though they were natural phenomena, isolating them, separating them from the consciousness that had constituted them. For Sartre, who had adopted Husserl's position as his own, consciousness was not a simple container of psychic "facts" nor was it some sort of mirror that passively reflected (or deformed) external reality; consciousness was, instead, fundamentally *intentional,* active, and had its own way of structuring sensory data and building up "realities" that, while depending upon that sense-information, presented specific characteristics that were all their own.

Sartre formalized the application of the phenomenological method to problems of psychology in three essays: *Imagination: A Psychological Critique* (1936), *The Emotions: Outline of a Theory* (1939), and *The Psychology of the Imagination* (1940). For Sartre, it was not a question of studying a given emotion or gathering data on specific emotional behaviors as a traditional psychologist would do, but rather of going to the fundamental structures of consciousness, those structures that allow and explain emotional phenomena. In his view, imagination and emotion were organized modes of consciousness, particular ways of relating to the world, of giving meaning to the experiences of life. Moreover, mental images were not simple "copies" or "repetitions" of external data, objects, and facts; on the contrary, the functioning of the imagination revealed the consciousness' fundamental property of standing at a distance from things, transcending things, and freely creating other realities – as artistic activity, for example, makes abundantly clear.

Because of the central importance that Husserl gave to the logical and gnoseological aspects of his work, however, Sartre soon grew away from him. For Sartre, what one had to do was to study the relationship between the real, existing human consciousness on the one hand and, on the other, the world of things to which the consciousness, by its very constitution, is always linked, but which it also feels limited and oppressed by. Following this line, Sartre moved increasingly close to Heidegger's ontological and existential position on these problems, until he arrived at last at a philosophical vision whose central idea was that of a "contradictory complementarity" between consciousness (the *for-itself*) and the world (the *in-itself*).

Sartre reformulated the fundamental idea of phenomenology – the *intentionality* of consciousness – as *transcendence toward* the world: consciousness transcends itself, constantly goes beyond itself toward the world of things. But though the world sustains and is the support for the intentional activity of consciousness, the world is not *reducible* to the consciousness; for consciousness, the world is the "other," the reality of things and facts – a solid, opaque reality that is given and gratuitous. The world of things, "facticity," is absurd and inexplicable; it is *there,* but it need not be there because there is nothing that explains it; it is contingent, yet it *is* there, it *does* exist. Or, rather, following Heidegger, it "ex-sists;" it emerges, it "stands out" to consciousness.

The same can be said of the human being: the human being is contingent because destined to die; could *not* exist, and yet *does* exist, *is there,* thrown into the world without having chosen to be; the human being is *in-situation,* in a particular time and place, with that particular body, in that particular society, there, questioning, "under an empty sky." And he uses the word "nausea" to describe that sensation of radical unease or anguish that consciousness feels in the face of the absurdity and contingency of everything that exists, and of existence itself once it has called into crisis, or "suspended" as Husserl would have it, habitual meanings and values.

In *Being and Nothingness: An Essay on Phenomenological Ontology* written in 1943, consciousness is described as standing in, maintaining, an almost unbearable tension with the world that surrounds it ("Being"), the world with which it must necessarily be in relation and yet with which it never feels fully in harmony. Consciousness, which is the absolute freedom to create the meanings of things, particular situations, and the world in general, is ceaselessly forced to make choices, to make distinctions regarding reality. By its very constitution, consciousness contains within itself *le néant,* "nothingness," in that it continually negates, annuls that which exists, projecting itself beyond that which is given, that which is already done, to create new plans, new projects, new possibilities.

In the unceasing labor of projection and self-projection that annuls and reconstructs the world, the human being is, by essence, his or her own possibilities; the constant choices, plans, and actions in which the human being engages give rise to and constantly put the individual's existence at stake, at risk. Therefore, what characterizes human reality is not some preconstituted essence, but rather, precisely, existence itself – the human being's incessant questioning of itself and the world, its freedom to choose among different possibilities and to choose how it will be, its plans and projects for the future, its being always "beyond itself."

It is precisely the freedom to choose, however, the absolute freedom that is the very essence of consciousness, that generates "anguish." In *Being and Nothingness,* following not only Heidegger but Kierkegaard as well, Sartre defined *anguish* as the sensation of vertigo that invades a person when he discovers his freedom and realizes that he and he alone is responsible for his own decisions and actions. Anguish (or "dread"), unlike fear, which is always connected to an object, has no specific reference but might be defined as "the fear of being afraid" or, as Kierkegaard put it, the "fear and trembling" before the indeterminacy and complexity of the alternatives, the choices that existence presents. It is in order to flee the anguish that accompanies freedom, in order to avoid the responsibility of choice, that individuals so frequently resort to those forms of self-deception that constitute "escape" ("fugue") and "excuse" or indulge in the hypocrisy of "dishonesty" or "bad faith," in which consciousness attempts to lie to itself, concealing from itself its motivations and masking and idealizing its purposes. This is the inauthentic mode of being of that bourgeoisie portrayed so mercilessly some years previously in Sartre's 1938 novel *Nausea* (*La Nausée*) and his 1939 collection of short stories *The Wall* (*Le Mur*).

Being contingent, however, consciousness, which is the basis of everything, is unable to find justification for itself either in the world or in itself. Consciousness, then, presents a duality – a paradox inescapable because it is *constitutive* of consciousness, providing a glimpse of an underlying indecipherability, a non-transparency: even while consciousness is the freedom to create new possibilities, the freedom to give meaning to the world, it can never form a *definitive* meaning, never arrive at the fixed crystallization of a value.

At the conclusion of *Being and Nothingness* Sartre says "the for-itself is *effectively* a perpetual project of founding itself *qua* being and a perpetual failure of this project."[31]

In summary, for the Sartre of *Being and Nothingness* the essence of human consciousness lies in the permanently frustrated and self-frustrated attempt to ground itself, to anchor itself. It is a "labor of Sisyphus," as Camus was to say, a perpetual doing and undoing, a commitment it is necessary to assume, but for which no recompense or hope whatever can be foreseen, and which only death, as the last "fact," will abruptly bring to an end. There may be rebellion and denunciation of "bad faith," but always under an "empty sky." *Being and Nothingness* offers no positive proposal, points out no direction in which one may move in order to escape the checkmate, the meaninglessness of existence. The book concludes with the assertion that "man is a useless passion," and with the admission that all possible choices are equivalent and always, in the final analysis, negative.

This posture of "atheistic existentialism," as it was called, grew so popular as to become almost a fad in the climate of

31. Sartre, *Being and Nothingness*, Philosophical Library, 617. Washington Square Press, 759.

disorientation and pessimism in which Europe found itself following the liberation. Sartre, who had taken part only marginally in the French resistance against the Nazis, "carrying some bags," as he himself put it, found his thought a dominant influence on the French philosophico-political scene, along with Marxism and Christian Humanism. Meanwhile, the international political picture was once more growing ominous, with the first symptoms of the cold war between the Soviet Union and the United States and renewed threats of conflict hanging over a divided Europe.

Thus, in the new postwar political climate and his own confrontation with Marxism, Sartre made a strong effort to reformulate his existentialism, placing greater emphasis on the ethical and political aspects of his system and its "intersubjective" and political implications. He recast existentialism as a humanist doctrine at the core of which were the human being and human freedom, and which, moreover, urged individuals to make a militant commitment to society and struggle against all forms of oppression and alienation.

A doctrine structured in that way might serve as a basis for building a new political force and for the opening of a "third way" between the Christian and Communist parties. In particular, Sartre addressed the French left, proposing existentialism as a philosophy of freedom that was more than a revolutionary and antibourgeois philosophy, and as an alternative to Marxism and its deterministic vision, which annulled the individual and the individual's uniqueness. Sartre considered Marxism, and especially its Leninist form, to be totally lacking in a coherent vision of humanity, totally lacking in a theory of the active subject.

It was with that intention, then, that in 1946 Sartre published *L'Existentialisme est un humanisme* (in English, *Existentialism*). This essay is a slightly modified text of a lecture he had given the previous year at the Club Maintenant in

Paris. The immediate purpose of the lecture was to respond to the distorted accusations against and misunderstandings of existentialism that were then circulating among both the right and the left. The adversaries of existentialism on the right claimed that it was a doctrine of the absurd, of nothingness, that it was materialist and atheistic, that it focused on the human being's crudest and most sordid aspects, and that interpersonal relations were portrayed in it as a sort of reciprocal torture. The adversaries of existentialism on the left, meanwhile, were describing it as a decadent theory, a typical product of that petit-bourgeois idealism that led only to paralysis and resignation and whose myopic subjectivism failed to take into account the real factors of oppression that acted on the human being – the various forms of social and economic domination exerted by capitalist society.

In light of this background, which we have reviewed in order to understand the philosophical and political environment in which Sartre then moved, let us look at how he presented and defended the thesis that existentialism is a humanism:

> I shall try today to answer these ... charges. Many people are going to be surprised at what is said here about humanism. We shall try to see in what sense it is to be understood. In any case, what can be said from the very beginning is that by existentialism we mean a doctrine which makes human life possible and, in addition, declares that every truth and every action implies a human setting and a human subjectivity (*Existentialism*, 12).

Sartre continues:

> Subjectivity of the individual is indeed our point of departure, and this for strictly philosophic reasons.... There can be no other truth to take off from than this: *I think; therefore, I exist.* There we have the absolute truth of con-

sciousness becoming aware of itself. Every theory which takes man out of the moment in which he becomes aware of himself is, at its very beginning, a theory which confounds truth, for outside the Cartesian *cogito,* all views are only probable, and a doctrine of probability which is not bound to a truth dissolves into thin air. In order to describe the probable, you must have a firm hold on the true. Therefore, before there can be any truth whatsoever, there must be an absolute truth; and this one is simple and easily arrived at; it's on everyone's doorstep; it's a matter of grasping it directly.

Secondly, this theory is the only one which gives man dignity, the only one which does not reduce him to an object (*Existentialism,* 42–43).

As distinct from what occurs in Cartesian philosophy, for Sartre the *cogito,* the "I think," led directly back to the world, to other human beings; thus:

[T]he man who becomes aware of himself through the *cogito* also perceives all others, and he perceives them as the condition of his own existence. He realizes that he can not be anything (in the sense that we say that someone is witty or nasty or jealous) unless others recognize it as such. In order to get any truth about myself, I must have contact with another person. The other is indispensable to my own existence, as well as to my knowledge about myself. This being so, in discovering my inner being I discover the other person at the same time, like a freedom placed in front of me which thinks and wills only for or against me. Hence, let us at once announce the discovery of a world which we shall call intersubjectivity; this is the world in which man decides what he is and what others are (*Existentialism,* 44–45).

Sartre next goes on to give the definition of the human being from the point of view of existentialism. In Sartre's view, all existentialists of whatever stripe, Christian or atheist, including Heidegger, concur in this: in the human being, *existence* precedes *essence*. To make this point clear, Sartre gives the following example:

> Let us consider some object that is manufactured, for example, a book or a paper-cutter: here is an object which has been made by an artisan whose inspiration came from a concept. He referred to the concept of what a paper-cutter is and likewise to a known method of production, which is part of the concept, something which is, by and large, a routine. Thus, the paper-cutter is at once an object produced in a certain way and, on the other hand, one having a specific use; and one can not postulate a man who produces a paper-cutter but does not know what it is used for. Therefore, let us say that, for the paper-cutter, essence – that is, the ensemble of both the production routines and the properties which enable it to be both produced and defined – precedes existence (*Existentialism*, 15–16).

In the Christian religion, Sartre continues, within which European thought has been formed, "[w]hen we conceive God as the Creator, He is generally thought of as a superior sort of artisan.... Thus, the concept of man in the mind of God is comparable to the concept of paper-cutter in the mind of the manufacturer, and, following certain techniques and a conception, God produces man, just as the artisan, following a definition and a technique, makes a paper-cutter.... In the eighteenth century, the atheism of the *philosophes* discarded the idea of God, but not so much for the notion that essence precedes existence" (*Existentialism*, 16–17).

Following this line of thought, Sartre says that man "has a human nature; this human nature, which is the concept of the human, is found in all men, which means that each man is a particular example of a universal concept, man" (*Existentialism*, 16–17).

Sartre continues:

[B]ut atheistic existentialism, which I represent, is more coherent. It states that if God does not exist, there is at least
one being in whom existence precedes essence, a being who
exists before he can be defined by any concept, and that this
being is man, or, as Heidegger says, human reality. What is
meant here by saying that existence precedes essence? It
means that, first of all, man exists, turns up, appears on the
scene, and, only afterwards, defines himself. If man, as the
existentialist conceives him, is indefinable, it is because at
first he is nothing. Only afterward will he be something, and
he himself will have made what he will be (*Existentialism,*
18).

Sartre goes on to clarify this thought still further:

Man is nothing else but what he makes of himself. Such is
the first principle of existentialism. It is also what is called
subjectivity, the name we are labeled with when charges are
brought against us. But what do we mean by this, if not that
man has a greater dignity than a stone or table? For we mean
that man first exists, that is, that man first of all is the being
who hurls himself toward a future and who is conscious of
imagining himself as being in the future. Man is at the start a
plan which is aware of itself; ... nothing exists prior to this
plan; ... man will be what he will have planned to be (*Existentialism,* 18–19).

Thus, the human being does not have a fixed or unchanging essence; the human essence is constructed upon existence, first as plan or project, that "hurling oneself toward
the future," and then as actions. Human beings are free to
be whatever they want to be, but in this process of self-
formation they have no moral rules to guide them.

Recalling one of the thinkers who inspired existentialism,
Sartre notes:

Dostoievski said, "If God didn't exist, everything would be
possible." That is the very starting point of existentialism.

> Indeed, everything is permissible if God does not exist, and as a result man is forlorn, because neither within him nor without does he find anything to cling to. He can't start making excuses for himself.
>
> If existence really does precede essence, there is no explaining things away by reference to a fixed and given human nature. In other words, there is no determinism, man is free, man is freedom. On the other hand, if God does not exist, we find no values or commands to turn to which legitimize our conduct. So, in the bright realm of values, we have no excuse behind us, nor justification before us. We are alone, with no excuses.
>
> That is the idea I shall try to convey when I say that man is condemned to be free. Condemned, because he did not create himself, yet, in other respects ... free; because, once thrown into the world, he is responsible for everything he does.... [m]an, with no support and no aid, is condemned every moment to invent man (*Existentialism*, 27–28).

According to what Heidegger had taught, then, man was alone and abandoned in the world; furthermore, he was forced to choose, and to construct himself through that choosing. The abandonment and the choosing are accompanied by *anguish*. It should be noted that in the attempt to recast existentialism as a humanism, Sartre found himself obliged to revise this point, giving a separate and distinct function to the concept of anguish that had had so much importance in his preceding philosophy.

In *Being and Nothingness* Sartre had described anguish as the sensation of terrible vertigo that comes over a person when he discovers that he is free and that he must take responsibility for his actions and his choices. But in *Existentialism,* the meaning of anguish for Sartre is transferred from the subjective to the intersubjective sphere. Anguish then becomes the feeling of "crushing responsibility" accompanying a choice that involves not only the individual but other human beings as well, or even all of humanity in the case of very important, radical decisions.

Here is how Sartre addresses this topic:

> When we say that man chooses his own self, we mean that every one of us does likewise; but we also mean by that that in making this choice he also chooses all men. In fact, in creating the man that we want to be, there is not a single one of our acts which does not at the same time create an image of man as we think he ought to be. To choose to be this or that is to affirm at the same time the value of what we choose, because we can never choose evil. We always choose the good, and nothing can be good for us without being good for all (*Existentialism*, 20).

It is on this foundation that Sartre constructs a social ethics of freedom: "[W]hen, in all honesty, I've recognized that man is a being in whom existence precedes essence, that he is a free being who, in various circumstances, can want only his freedom, I have at the same time recognized that I can want only the freedom of others" (*Existentialism*, 54–55).

Thus, Sartre's ethics is not based on the thing chosen but rather on the honesty or "authenticity" of the choice.[32] In contrast to his assertions in *Being and Nothingness*, now not all behaviors are equally lacking in meaning for Sartre. Although he reiterates that in order to act it is *not* necessary to have hope, now he also says that action is *not* necessarily gratuitous, absurd, or without foundation. In fact, even though no sweeping and definitive morality exists, even though every individual is free to construct his or her own

32. This concept and its negative – dishonesty, inauthenticity, "bad faith" – are translated using these different words by Sartre's various translators; we have included the range of renderings to make these passages more recognizable for readers of Sartre in English, no matter which English versions they have read. [Trans.]

morality within the situation he or she lives, by choosing between the various possibilities that present themselves it is
nonetheless possible for the individual to make moral judgments. This moral judgment is based on the recognition of
freedom (one's own and that of others) and of dishonesty or
bad faith – that is, self-deception:

> [O]ne can judge...that certain choices are based on error and
> others on truth. If we have defined man's situation as a free
> choice, with no excuses and no recourse, every man who
> takes refuge behind the excuse of his passions, every man
> who sets up a determinism, is a dishonest man [is in "bad
> faith"]...[But s]uppose someone says to me, "What if I want
> to be dishonest [act in bad faith]?" I'll answer, "There's no
> reason for you not to be, but I'm saying that that's what you
> are, and that the strictly coherent attitude is that of honesty."
> ... I can bring moral judgment to bear (*Existentialism*, 52–
> 53).

Let us now consider in what sense existentialism, which is
at bottom an attempt to deduce all the consequences of a coherent atheism, can be said to be a humanism:

> [M]an is constantly outside of himself; in projecting himself,
> in losing himself outside of himself, he makes for man's exist-
> ing; and, on the other hand, it is by pursuing transcendent
> goals that he is able to exist; man, being this state of passing-
> beyond, and seizing upon things only as they bear upon this
> passing-beyond, is at the heart, at the center of this passing-
> beyond. There is no universe other than a human universe,
> the universe of human subjectivity. This connection between
> transcendency, as a constituent element of man – not in the
> sense that God is transcendent, but in the sense of passing
> beyond – and subjectivity, in the sense that man is not closed
> in on himself but is always present in a human universe, is
> what we call existentialist humanism. Humanism, because
> we remind man that there is no law-maker other than him-

self, and that in his forlornness he will decide by himself; because we point out that man will fulfill himself as man, not in turning toward himself, but in seeking outside of himself a goal which is just this liberation, just this particular fulfillment (*Existentialism*, 59–60).

These are, in brief, the fundamental ideas of existentialist humanism as Sartre formulated them in 1945–46. But in the years that followed, in a difficult journey that led Sartre first to be a "fellow traveler" of the French Communist Party and then later, following the Soviet invasion of Hungary in 1956, to break openly with it, Sartre was to subject his philosophical position to constant reappraisal and, sometimes, profound changes. Along the way he also reformulated several of the ideas he had set forth in *Existentialism*. For instance, after his encounter with Marxism, which stimulated him to undertake a more profound analysis of social reality, Sartre came to stress the idea of a freedom that was not absolute but "conditioned" by an ensemble of social and cultural factors.

He himself admitted that the radical antithesis he had drawn between absolute freedom and equally absolute bad faith in his 1943 *Being and Nothingness* had been inspired by the climate of war, in which there seemed to be no gray, but only black and white, no alternative but being fully "for" or fully "against." But after the war came the true experience – the experience of *society* – that is, the experience of a complex and ambiguous reality charged with nuances and gradations, where the relationship between the determining situation and free will, between conditioning and choice, was neither clear nor direct. In an interview given to the *New Left Review* in 1969, Sartre offered the following definition of freedom: "I believe," he said, "that a man can always make something out of what is made of him. This is the limit I would today accord to freedom: the small movement which makes of a totally conditioned social being someone who does not render back completely what his conditioning has given him."[33]

Even with this more limited definition of freedom, Sartre did not renounce the central theme of all his philosophy, that freedom is constitutive of human consciousness. In 1974, six years before his death, now nearly blind, in a debate with the *gauchistes* (leftists) of the May 1968 Paris student revolt, Sartre reaffirmed that human beings are never wholly identifiable with their conditioning, that alienation is possible precisely because the individual is free, because the human being is not a thing.[34]

This is, in brief summary, the philosophical road traveled by Sartre, a difficult journey with many changes and self-critiques but always exhibiting a certain "constancy" as well. All along Sartre was forced to respond to attacks from the hypocritical bourgeoisie and Christians on one side and Marxists on the other, but ironically, when he attempted to give his philosophy a humanist formulation, the most profound and radical criticism came from precisely the man who had inspired so many aspects of Sartre's existentialism, Martin Heidegger.

33. Sartre, "Itinerary of a Thought: Interview with Jean-Paul Sartre," 45.
34. Sartre, Gavi, and Victor, *On a raison de se révolter: discusions.*

4. Heidegger's Critique of Metaphysical Humanism

MARTIN HEIDEGGER (1889–1976) graduated from and began his teaching career at the University of Freiburg in Germany. In 1916 a crucial period in his philosophical formation began when Edmund Husserl, recently appointed to the chair in philosophy, chose Heidegger as his assistant. Husserl was already a well known and widely respected philosopher, and his phenomenology had developed into a growing movement that was generating considerable interest. In the close collaboration that ensued between the two men, Heidegger made decisive contributions to the development of phenomenology, not only through his own researches but also through his influence on the direction of Husserl's work. Husserl sometimes described the school of phenomenology of that period in Freiburg in this way: "Phenomenology is myself and Heidegger, and nobody else."

In 1927 Heidegger (now a professor of philosophy at the University of Marburg) published his fundamental work *Being and Time,* dedicating it to Husserl. But this work also signaled a break between the two men, which became obvious on the occasion of their failed attempt to coauthor the article on phenomenology for the *Encyclopædia Britannica.* And the break between them also marked a schism in the school of phenomenology itself, as Husserl made plain in 1931 when he attacked what he called Heidegger's "philosophy of existence."

In 1928 Heidegger succeeded Husserl to the chair of philosophy at the University of Freiburg. At his inaugural, Heidegger gave a paper that would come to be one of his best known and most controversial works, "What Is Metaphysics?" In 1933, when Nazism achieved political ascendancy in Germany, Husserl, a Jew, was expelled from the faculty of the university and Heidegger was appointed chancellor. One month later Heidegger joined the National Socialist Party, though his membership seems to have lasted less than a year, for in 1934 he resigned his position, refusing to obey orders from the government to expel two anti-Nazi colleagues from the faculty. From that time on Heidegger no longer involved himself in politics, entering instead into a period of withdrawal and silence, and not publishing due to government opposition. He did continue to teach at the university, though he was under constant surveillance by the SS.

Heidegger's brief membership in the Nazi Party always thereafter cast him in a sinister light; it was a stigma that hindered a more widespread understanding of his philosophy and the revolution in Western thought that it produced.

When the war came to an end, the leadership of the occupying forces forbade Heidegger to teach until 1951, but in 1946 the prohibition was lifted and he began to teach again, at first privately. During this period he also published a large number of essays, most written during the years of silence that had followed the publication of *Being and Time*. These essays testify to a turn in Heidegger's thought, what has been called a "second phase" in his philosophy, and this new direction appears explicitly in his "Letter on Humanism," published in 1947. We will return to this essay in some detail shortly, but first we will briefly look at *Being and Time*.

Being and Time begins with an epigraph from Plato's *Sophistes* that clearly illustrates the problem at hand: "For manifestly you have long been aware of what you mean when you use the expression 'being.' We, however, who used to think we understood it, have now become perplexed."[35] Heidegger asks himself whether the word *being* is better understood today than in Plato's time, whether it is clear to us what we mean when we use it. The answer he gives is that it is not, and that in fact we have forgotten about the problem itself – for the fact that we do not understand the meaning of the word *being* creates no perplexity in us whatever; we use it constantly but never pause to analyze it, never ask ourselves what it means. We say "such-and-such *is*..." and continue on with a series of predicates that define the object under consideration; we debate whether a thing is this way or that way, this or that, yet never examine the word *is*. Since it is the "most universal and emptiest of all concepts," the concept applied to all entities (things, animals, vegetables, ourselves, and so on), the concept of Being apparently "resists every attempt at definition" (H 2). Its meaning is lost in common use.

In its long history, philosophy has given differing answers to the fundamental question of *being,* and Heidegger says that he does not pretend to give a new one. In view of the fact that the problem itself seems to have been forgotten, what Heidegger wishes to do, rather, is to reawaken an understanding of the meaning of the question itself. The fact that one asks oneself what an entity *is,* that one asks "What is *X?*" presupposes a vague, average understanding of the being of entities (H 4). And it is precisely on the basis of that understanding that one also asks oneself about *being.* Therefore, a study of the meaning of Being should begin from this entity that appears to occupy a privileged position – that is, should involve a preliminary clarification of the being of the human being.

35. Heidegger, *Being and Time,* 19 (H 1). From this point on, page number references will be given to the original German text as is standard in quoting Heidegger because of the difficulty in translating his terminology; thus, page numbers will appear as "H [p.]" [Trans.]

Yet one cannot inquire into the question of the being – or essence – of the human being in the same way that one investigates the being of other entities. In traditional philosophy, when one speaks of the "essence" or "nature" of an entity, one is referring to the ensemble of specific characteristics inherent in that entity, and without which it would not be what it is. For Heidegger, however, the human being is never an entity that is definitive, fixed, completed; the human being's most characteristic mode of being is, rather, *existing* – a continual being in relationship to possibilities, a continual going beyond the given. In other words, the human being, "that entity we always are," does not present itself in the mode of reality, the mode of objectivity; rather, the human being presents itself as *existence,* which is possibility, *coming-into-Being* or *potentiality for Being.* To say that the *essence* of the human being is *existence* is equivalent to saying that the human being possesses no essence in the traditional sense at all, no essence given or defined as it is for things.

For Heidegger, then, between the human being and other entities there exists a radical difference in essence that must not be overlooked. If it is – if the human being is reduced to "just another" entity and studied as "just another" entity, as a *thing,* in the way that human sciences such as anthropology, biology, and psychology treat the human being as an *object* – then the human being's most particular and constitutive characteristics are lost. In turn, this difference becomes the point of departure for the *existential analysis* that Heidegger believes will shed light (little by little, with the progressive deepening and unveiling that are characteristic of the phenomenological method) on the structures that constitute the being of the human being.

Thus, out of the first level of analysis emerges the notion that the essence of the human being lies in its *existence.* But this existence does not occur in the abstract but rather concretely, in a world constituted by things and other human beings. Accordingly, for Heidegger existence is fundamentally *Being-in-the-world*. He designates the human essence by the term *Dasein*, which literally means "existence," though he decomposes the word into its parts, making it *Da-sein* or *being-there*. Thus, Heidegger emphasizes the character of human reality as Being-in-the-world and *opening to* the world.

But what are we to understand by the term *world*? One of the central tenets of Heidegger's philosophy is that the world is not simply the sum of all possible entities as things-in-themselves, endowed with *objective* reality. For Heidegger, the reason philosophy has never managed to satisfactorily explain life or history is precisely that it has always conceived of reality as *simple presence,* or better (using a term already common in the language of both science and daily life), *objectivity.* This view presupposes that on one side there is a subject who is separate and apart and who observes things, and on the other side there are things, each of which possesses a particular and unique nature *in-itself,* which the subject strives to apprehend through a gaze, a way of seeing that is as pure and disinterested as possible, as the exact sciences attempt to do. But an analysis of the meaning of the term *world* shows that initially things present themselves to us not as objects separate from ourselves, as *things-in-themselves,* endowed with objective existence. Rather, in our experience things are above all instruments or instrumentalities, in the sense that we always *include* them in some way in our lives, we have a purpose for them, we refer them to a "plan" or "project." The world is, then, the horizon within which we use and give meaning to the things we encounter there, those things we are able to *put to use.* In that sense, the world is a structure constitutive of human reality.

For Heidegger, human *opening* to the world occurs through three basic modalities: emotion or "mood," "understanding," and "discourse." As one way of opening, the human being always experiences its own Being-in-the-world within a certain emotional stance, what Heidegger calls "mood." Thus, the human being's relationship to things is never neutral, its attitude is never that of a "pure subject," rather, the human being "*feels* itself" in the world. Therefore, the individual's emotional situation or "mood" is an *apprehension,* a *pre-comprehension,* of the world. Nevertheless, that "mood" is not fully under the individual's control; the affective tonality that determines the person's mode of relationship to things is not fully subject to that person's control. It is through this *opening* that human beings discover that the fundamental aspect of their existence eludes them. Their emotional situation or "mood" confronts human beings with their own inexplicability and finitude, with the fact of their being *thrown,* abandoned, into the world (H 135ff.).

As a second way of opening, human beings always have a certain *comprehension* or *understanding* of the world in the sense that they have a knowledge of or familiarity with a totality of meanings, even before encountering the objects that come into their awareness. As *coming-into-Being* or *potentiality for Being,* what is constitutive of the human being in the world is "projecting," throwing forward, planning (H 145ff.), and their knowledge of things is always an interpretation, an inclusion of these things within a human plan or "project." Thus, "understanding" is not something that consists of knowing things "as they are," "in-themselves," but rather is always the expression of an inescapable *relationship* with things. And as such, as part of a project, our understanding/interpretation of the world is always subject to change and development.

Finally, as the third mode of opening to the world, "discourse" articulates and concretizes the other two, mood and understanding.

Through these three fundamental modes of opening to the world, human beings "care" or have "concern"[36] for things, other human beings, and themselves. Caring-for, dedicating-oneself-to, is the *being* of human reality as existence.

Taking the analysis further, Heidegger finds in *temporality* the meaning of this "care" or "concern." In other words, what makes it possible and comprehensible for a human being to enter into relationship with objects, to give them meaning, to include them in a project, lies in temporality. Heidegger puts the idea this way:

> Such concern [solicitude, etc.], as concernfully reckoning up, planning, preventing, or taking precautions, always says (whether audibly or not) that something is to happen *"then,"* that something else is to be attended to *"beforehand,"* that what has failed or eluded us *"on that former occasion"* is something that we must *"now"* make up for (H 406, italics in English edition).

For Heidegger, however, *temporality* is not "time" as the word is generally understood. In *Being and Time* Heidegger carries out an extraordinarily profound analysis of the common understanding of "time," which is ordinarily seen as a succession of "instants" within which events are "dated." Thus, time is normally conceived of as a line (composed of instants that are the points of the line) stretching infinitely into both the past and the future. The instant-point is always taken to be *now,* and past and future are only understood based on the experience of the present. But the *now* of the

36. "Care" or "concern" is also translated as "solicitude," see, for example, *n., H* 121. [Trans.]

present is always experienced as it recedes into the past and extends toward the future, and thus *now* is necessarily also "a little while ago" and "in just a little while." Furthermore, if the past is understood as a function of the present, as a function of the *now,* then it is a *no-longer-now;* and the future, correspondingly, is a *not-yet-now.*

The image of time as the infinite succession of instant-points, of *nows,* arises when the "nows" of the present (which possess the characteristics we have noted) are projected into the past and the future. This is the way Heidegger describes the common conception of time and the sense of its appearance:

> It is held that time presents itself proximally as an uninter-rupted sequence of "nows." Every "now," moreover, is al-ready either a "just-now" or a "forthwith." If in characteriz-ing time we stick primarily and exclusively *to such a sequence,* then in principle neither beginning nor end can be found in it. Every last "now," as *"now,"* is always *already* a "forthwith" that is no longer; thus it is time in the sense of the "no-longer-now" – in the sense of the past. Every first "now" is a "just-now" that is not yet; thus it is time in the sense of the "not-yet-now" – in the sense of the "future." Hence time is endless "on both sides." This thesis becomes possible only on the basis of an orientation *towards a free-floating "in-itself" of a course of "nows" which is present-at-hand....* If one directs one's glance toward Being-present-at-hand and not-Being-present-at-hand, and thus "thinks" the sequence of "nows" through "to the end," then an end can never be found. In *this* way of *thinking* time through to the end, one *must* always *think* more time; from this one infers that time *is* infinite.

But wherein are grounded this leveling-off of world-time and this covering-up of temporality? In the Being of Dasein itself, which we have ... interpreted as *care.* Thrown and falling, Dasein is proximally and for the most part lost in that with which it concerns itself. In this lostness, however, Dasein's fleeing in the face of that authentic existence which has been characterized as "anticipatory resoluteness" [in the face of death] has made itself known; and this is a fleeing which covers up. In this concernful fleeing lies a fleeing *in the face of* death – that is, a looking-away *from* the end of Being-in-the-world [existence] (H 424, punctuation as in the English edition).

In other words, for Heidegger the reason we have constructed this illusory image of temporality, the "meaning" of that construct, lies in our attempt to evade ("look away from" or "flee") the problem of death. Of all the possibilities that present themselves to the human being – an entity that is, as we have seen, fundamentally *coming-into-Being* – death is the only one that is unavoidable, and therefore fundamental to and constitutive of human existence.

Existence, Heidegger says, is thus fundamentally *Being-toward-death*. In the face of the anxiety, the Angst, produced by the nothingness of death, the human being has two possible avenues: the first is to lose oneself in the world, to abandon oneself to the quotidian banality of, the *concern with,* projects constantly done and then demolished or undone, projects achieved or frustrated. In choosing this alternative, one creates for oneself the illusion of time as an infinite succession of "nows," thereby putting off the dark knowledge that one's own time is necessarily finite.

The present, the "now," is always a "meanwhile," always stands in relation to some present object that is part of a project. One thus comes to see entities as things-present and to see oneself as an I-thing. The dimensions of this form of inauthentic life are "idle talk," "curiosity," and misunderstanding or "vagueness;" the "I myself" becomes depersonalized, a vague "somebody" in the impersonal words *one, they,* or *people* of such impersonal expressions as "they say" or "it is believed" or "people do," because in this way the death that the subject avoids or flees becomes *the death of others,* and never the subject's own. It is precisely out of the statement "one dies" or "people die" that all other *one*s or *they*s or *people*s are born. We see, then, that the day-to-day relationship between the human being (who rejects his or her Being-toward-death) and the world is marked by this inauthenticity, which Heidegger calls *thrownness,* as in having "fallen" or "thrown-awayness."

Heidegger contrasts fallen or thrown-existence with the second of the human being's two avenues of life in the face of death-anxiety: the possibility of achieving an authentic mode of existence. The authentic mode of existence can be achieved only through an "anticipatory resoluteness" in the face of death. In this resoluteness, the human being consciously accepts and takes on the possibility of death as that possibility most centrally human. Arriving at the core of the anxiety over not-being, one opens oneself to authentically living all the other possibilities of existence. Discovering, without masks or self-delusion, that one *is-toward-death* and has been *thrown* into the world, also means discovering what one *has always been.* That is, one can authentically *have-been* only insofar as one discovers oneself in one's future. In a sense, then, the past arises out of the future. In this way, in the authentic project the human being anticipates itself or, as Heidegger says, "comes-toward" itself and, in that "ek-stasis" as he comes to call it, defines the past and the present. Thus, *"the primary phenomenon of primordial and authentic temporality is the future"* (H 329, italics original).

Heidegger urges us not to consider temporality as something that occurs in time as time is commonly understood. This tendency, like the common understanding of the concepts of past and future, derives from our illusory concept of time:

> By the term "futural," we do not here have in view a "now" which has *not yet* become "actual" and which sometime *will be* for the first time. We have in view the coming in which Dasein, in its ownmost potentiality-for-Being, comes towards itself. Anticipation makes Dasein *authentically* futural, and in such a way that the anticipation itself is possible only in so far as Dasein, *as being,* is always coming towards itself – that is to say, in so far as it is futural in its Being in general (H 325; quotation marks and italics original).

To put the issue in simpler terms, although the human being has always been a project toward the future, it is in their conscious acceptance of death that human beings come to see their anticipation or projection into the future (using these words in their traditional ways). Here we are not dealing with a cause that produces an effect, but rather with an un-veiling, a transcending of oneself, an arrival at being that which always has been, for *"the primary meaning of existentiality is the future"* (H 327). This does not mean, as the naive way of thinking about time would have it, that the future "comes before" the present, in the sense of a "before" and an "after." Present-past-future are, Heidegger says, co-original and form a structural unity.

Being and Time was never finished. The original plan was for two parts of three sections each. Heidegger wrote only the first two sections of the first part which, as we have seen, analyze, respectively, human existence and its meaning, which is time; the third section, which was to have been titled *Time and Being* and which was to treat the central problem of the "meaning of being in general" was never written. Heidegger himself later explained that he had not been able to complete *Being and Time* "for reasons of language," since the language he had available was, at bottom, the traditional language of philosophy, which was marked by an original error that prevented it from being able to express the meaning of Being. That is, in Heidegger's view the entire history of Western thought, beginning with Plato and Aristotle, has conceived entities as *simple-presence,* and this has obscured the connection not only between the three temporal degrees of past, present, and future, but also between being and time. Within this horizon, the human being's relationship with entities has taken on the forms of an inauthentic and thrown-away existence, and so the language that has expressed, and still expresses, this relationship is necessarily marked by a forgetfulness, an oblivion of being. Therefore, being cannot be expressed in the language of traditional ontology, the language of metaphysics. It is for this reason that after *Being and Time,* reflection on language would come to occupy an increasingly central position in Heidegger's philosophy.

Nevertheless, the oblivion of being that marks the entire history of Western metaphysics cannot be considered simply a philosophical error. Indeed, if that has been the way Being has manifested itself to Being-there, to human existence in the world throughout the history of the West, it is because that is the way Being *is* for Being-there, for the human being in this cultural tradition. It has not been "error" that has been operating, therefore, but rather Destiny. In the Destiny of the West, Being is manifested by its covering, its hiding of itself. It is within this horizon that the meaning of technology becomes clear. The technological world, in which all things are instruments or instrumentalities, in which there are only entities, in which Being has been obscured and completely forgotten, is the most complete expression of Western thought and, at the same time, the point of arrival at a mode of expression of Being.

As we see clearly in these ideas, which belong to the "second phase" of Heidegger's philosophy (which succeeded the turn in his thinking after *Being and Time*), the terms of the relationship between human existence in the world, Being-there (*Da-sein*), and Being are now inverted. It is no longer the human being who inquires into or investigates Being and opens himself or herself to it; rather, it is Being that opens itself to the human being. And language is the new center of this relationship, though we must note that the one who speaks is no longer the human being, but Being. And existence, which had been defined as Being-in-the-world and Being-toward-death is now, in the "Letter on Humanism," defined as: "[The] standing in the lighting [*Lichtung*] of Being I call the ek-sistence of man."[37]

In this existential location, wherein the light of Being may begin to be seen, the human being hears the language of Being. And yet, as a well-known interpreter of Heidegger has pointed out, this "'voice of Being,' this 'non-spoken word,' this ontological language is no longer the bearer of human meanings; it is a sort of sacred language or mysterious symbol, a sort of revelation of Being in the absence of all human words. The philosopher, in the current sense of the term, should keep silent; it is the poet and the 'thinker' who will replace him. They have the word, or rather the word has them. The poet, confidant of Being, having learned to 'exist in that which has no name,' is able '*to name* the sacred.' As for the thinker, he is able '*to speak* Being.'"[38]

---

37. Heidegger, "Letter on Humanism," 204. Sometimes translated as "clearing of Being." Hereafter cited as "Letter." From this point on in his writings, Heidegger will write "ek-sistence" instead of "existence" and "Seyn" instead of "Sein" to emphasize the new meaning of these terms.

38. Thévenaz, *What Is Phenomenology?*, 62. Hereafter cited as *Phenomenology*.

With this conception of Being and language Heidegger consciously locates himself at the terminus of Western thought and ideally reconnects – in a leap backward over all metaphysics from Plato on – with the beginnings of that thought, the ancient pre-Socratics, who wrote "in poetry" and "*spoke* Being as one religiously recites a sacred formula" (*Phenomenology,* 63).

After this brief presentation of Heidegger's thought, let us now examine the position he takes with respect to humanism, which is the area of greatest interest to us in the context of the present work.

The publication in 1946 of Sartre's *Existentialism (L'Existentialisme est un humanisme)* was the cause of heated debate and profound controversy. At that time Jean Baufret, a French philosopher, wrote to Heidegger, asking him a series of questions about humanism, among them "how to give meaning once again to the word 'humanism,'" a word that both Christians and Marxists were then claiming for themselves and to which Sartrean existentialism had also laid claim.

Heidegger responded to these questions in a work entitled "Letter on Humanism," which was published, with some corrections, in 1947. In this work Heidegger traces the history of the idea of humanism from Greek antiquity to the present, reconstructing the various meanings that have been attributed to the word and the idea. Each of these meanings, noted Heidegger, is derived from a prior determination of what it means to be human – that is, what the *essence* of "the human being" is. It is clearly the definition of this essence that draws the line between the human and the inhuman.

The first humanism in history, Heidegger said, was that which arose in Rome in the time of the Republic. There the Roman who had incorporated Greek *learning* was the "human," in contrast to the uneducated "barbarian." The ideal of that humanism, then, was *humanitas,* the Latin translation of the Greek word *paideia,* "education." That Roman humanism was thus linked to the education imparted in the philosophical schools of late Greek civilization. Toward the end of the Middle Ages, Italian humanism, which was an express attempt to reestablish connections with Greece and Rome, would adopt that same humanistic ideal, though in that case the "barbarian" against whom the "human" was contrasted was the person of the Middle Ages. Every current of thought since the Renaissance that has taken the Greek and Roman civilizations as a model has also adopted this conception of humanism.

Other humanisms (Marxist, Christian, and Sartrean or existentialist humanisms) in no way return to antiquity, but each one instead determines the essence of humanity or humanness in its own way. Thus, "Marx demands that 'man's humanity' be recognized and acknowledged. He finds it in 'society.' 'Social' man is for him 'natural' man. In 'society' the 'nature' of man, that is, the totality of 'natural needs' (food, clothing, reproduction, economic sufficiency) is equably secured" ("Letter," 200).

The Christian humanist "sees the humanity of man...in contradistinction to *Deitas.* He is the man of the history of redemption who as a 'child of God' hears and accepts the call of the Father in Christ. Man is not of this world, since the 'world,' thought in terms of Platonic theory, is only a temporary passage to the beyond" ("Letter," 200).

For Sartrian existentialism, Heidegger says, man has no determined, specific essence; essence is constructed in existence through choice.

But, says Heidegger:

However different these forms of humanism may be in purpose and in principle, in the mode and means of their respective realizations, and in the form of their teaching, they nonetheless all agree in this, that the *humanitas* of *homo humanus* is determined with regard to an already established interpretation of nature, history, world, and the ground of the world, that is, of beings as a whole.

Every humanism is either grounded in a metaphysics or is itself made to be the ground of one. Every determination of the essence of man that already presupposes an interpretation of being without asking about the truth of Being, whether knowingly or not, is metaphysical ("Letter," 201–202).

Thus, for Heidegger, all these conceptions of humanism present the same underlying flaw: they are all metaphysical or construct a metaphysics. And we have seen how he includes in this category all Western thought, from Plato and Aristotle onward.

Metaphysics reduces the reality of an entity to a *simple-presence,* apprehends it only in the temporal dimension of the present. And in addition, metaphysics assumes the being of the entity, yet neither inquires into it nor *knows* it. As a consequence, metaphysics rests on a foundation that is unknown to it; the same thing necessarily happens with *all* metaphysical humanisms, both ancient and modern. They presuppose that the essence of the human being is self-evident, needing no discussion, because "Man is considered to be the *animal rationale.* This definition is not simply the Latin translation of the Greek *zoon logon echon,* but rather a metaphysical interpretation of it" ("Letter," 202). This definition is itself a type of metaphysics, an interpretation: it places the human being within the dimension of animality and then adds the epithet "rational," which is understood, according to the various philosophical systems, as *soul,* or *mind,* or *spirit,* or *thinking subject,* or *person,* and so forth. Clearly, these say things that are true about the human species, but they conceive its essence in too limited a way. "Metaphysics," says Heidegger, "thinks of man on the basis of *animalitas* and does not think in the direction of his *humanitas*" ("Letter," 204).

Heidegger contrasts this restrictive conception of the human essence with his own vision of Being, from which alone humankind can derive its appropriate foundation. As we have already noted, the conception of the relationship between the human being and Being that is proposed in the "Letter on Humanism" belongs to the "second phase" of Heidegger's thought. The essence of humankind is now its "ek-sistence," which is understood to be its "standing in the lighting [clearing] of Being" ("Letter," 204). Precisely because the human being dwells in proximity to Being, it is radically different from other living beings.

Here is how Heidegger formulates this concept:

> Ek-sistence can be said only of the essence of man, that is, only of the human way "to be." For as far as our experience shows, only man is admitted to the destiny of ek-sistence. Therefore ek-sistence can also never be thought of as a specific kind of living creature among others – granted that man is destined to think the essence of his Being and not merely to give accounts of the nature and history of his constitution and activities ("Letter," 204).

> Of all the beings that are, presumably the most difficult to think about are living creatures, because on the one hand they are in a certain way most closely related to us, and on the other are at the same time separated from our ek-sistent essence by an abyss. However, it might also seem as though the essence of divinity is closer to us than what is foreign in other living creatures, closer, namely, in an essential distance which however distant is nonetheless more familiar to our ek-sistent essence than is our appalling and scarcely conceivable bodily kinship with the beast ("Letter," 206).

We see that for Heidegger the human being is much closer to the divine, to Being understood as pure *transcendens,*
than to other living species. The fundamental expression of
this closeness is language. It is, then, on the basis of this
closeness and not on the basis of animality that human
essence ought to be thought of. In Heidegger's thought, the
word *ek-sistence,* with which he defines humanity's essence,
has nothing in common with the word *existence* as that
word is used in the metaphysical tradition. There existence
means "actuality," "the reality of the thing," in contrast to
its essence understood as logical possibility, as ideal exem-
plarity.

And for Heidegger, Sartre, too, is a part of that metaphysical tradition:

> Sartre expresses the basic tenet of existentialism in this way:
> Existence precedes essence. In this statement he is taking *ex-
> istentia* and *essentia* according to their metaphysical mean-
> ing, which from Plato's time on has said that *essentia* pre-
> cedes *existentia.* Sartre reverses this statement. But the rever-
> sal of a metaphysical statement remains a metaphysical
> statement. With it he stays with metaphysics in oblivion of
> the truth of Being ("Letter," 208).

Therefore, Sartrean existentialism has nothing to do with
Heidegger's philosophy. In another passage ("Letter," 213–
14), Heidegger inverts Sartre's phrase *précisément nous
sommes sur un plan où il y a seulement des hommes* (we are
precisely in a situation where there are only human beings)
to read *précisément nous sommes sur un plan où il y a prin-
cipalement l'Être* (we are precisely in a situation where principally there is Being).[39] For Heidegger, the plan or "situa-

---

39. Sartre's phrase is from *L'Existentialisme est un humanisme.* Paris:
Nagel, 1970, 36.

tion" about which Sartre is talking is precisely Being. The two philosophies are radically divergent.

For Heidegger, then, very little remains of the so-called "humanisms" once one has perceived and denounced the metaphysical roots that have determined their impoverishment and loss of meaning. Yet such a denunciation is not without a value of its own, for it allows the human essence to be conceived in a more "original" way – as *ek-sistence,* as the living of humankind in proximity to Being.

But, Heidegger asks, should this new way of thinking, which "contradicts all previous humanism" yet "in no way advocates the inhuman" ("Letter," 225) itself be called a "humanism"? "Or," asks Heidegger, "should thinking, by means of open resistance to 'humanism,' risk a shock that could for the first time cause perplexity concerning the *humanitas* of *homo humanus* and its basis? In this way it could awaken a reflection – if the world-historical moment did not itself already compel such a reflection – that thinks not only about man but also about the 'nature' of man, not only about his nature but even more primordially about the dimension in which the essence of man, determined by Being itself, is at home" ("Letter," 225).

This reflection on the human essence is fundamental, for it is only on the basis of comprehending that "essence" that a human being can construct his or her future ("Letter," 203–204). Yet restoring meaning to the word *humanism* cannot be an abstract operation; a more primary and original experience of the human essence is necessary. Traditional humanisms have failed in their objective: the modern human being feels alienated, homeless, without a country (this alienation, though, cannot be thought of in Marxist terms, but rather in terms of distance from Being).

A drawing nearer to forgotten Being is, then, the only possible avenue for extracting humanity from the situation of alienation and estrangement in which we find ourselves. In that *rapprochement* lies the Destiny of the West. This is the way Heidegger puts it: "[The] West [should not be] thought regionally as the Occident in contrast to the Orient, nor merely as Europe, but rather world-historically out of nearness to the source" ("Letter," 218). And again:

> The homeland of this historical dwelling is nearness to Being. In such nearness, if at all, a decision may be made as to whether and how God and the gods withhold their presence and the night remains, whether and how the day of the holy dawns, whether and how in the upsurgence of the holy an epiphany of God and the gods can begin anew. But the holy, which alone is the essential sphere of divinity, which in turn alone affords a dimension for the gods and for God, comes to radiate only when Being itself beforehand and after extensive preparation has been illuminated and is experienced in its truth. Only thus does the overcoming of homelessness begin from Being, a homelessness in which not only man but the essence of man stumbles aimlessly about ("Letter," 218).

This is, in brief synthesis, Heidegger's thought in regard to humanism. In the "Letter on Humanism" he has performed on traditional conceptions of humanism the same labor of deconstruction, of nullification, that he had performed on philosophy. For Heidegger, the vision that the metaphysical humanisms hold of the human being is insufficient – harmful, even – and so must be completely dismantled.

We should recall that if Heidegger rejected traditional humanism, it was because traditional humanism does not sufficiently realize the *humanitas* of humanity. But Heidegger does not say in what way it is possible to bring about this new experience of the human essence; he simply shows the need of that experience and states, generically, that it is for the West to bring it to realization. But it is for Being, and not the human being, to open itself, and in the forms that are appropriate to it. With respect to those forms, humanity plays no part; humanity can only prepare itself, in silence, for the revelation of Being.

5. Philosophical Anti-Humanism

5.1 Structuralism and Claude Lévi-Strauss

OF MODERN currents of thought, structuralism has taken perhaps the most determinedly anti-humanist stance. The name structuralism denotes a philosophical current that arose during the 1960s, especially in France, although it was neither a philosophical school nor a homogeneous movement at all, but rather, as others have pointed out, a "way of thinking" that linked quite distinct figures from a wide spectrum of fields in the human sciences, including anthropology (Claude Lévi-Strauss), literary criticism (Roland Barthes), Freudian psychoanalysis (Jacques Lacan), historiography (Michel Foucault), as well as philosophical currents such as Marxism (Louis Althusser).

However heterogeneous this group of scholars may have been, they were united in their rejection of the subjectivism, historicism, and humanism that were central to the interpretations of phenomenology and existentialism articulated by Jean-Paul Sartre and Marcel Merleau-Ponty in the years after World War II, interpretations that came to dominate French philosophy during that period. Employing a method in sharp contrast to that of Sartre and Merleau-Ponty, the structuralists tended to study the human being from outside, as though it were any natural phenomenon, "the way one would study ants" (as Lévi-Strauss was to say), and not from within, by studying consciousness. With this approach, which imitated the methods of the physical sciences, the structuralists attempted to develop research strategies that would throw light on the constant, systematic relationships that they believed existed within human behavior, individual and collective, and that they called "structures." These structures were not obvious or superficial relationships, however, but "deep" structures, for the most part not consciously perceived, yet which limited and constrained human action. Independent of the object of study, structuralist research tended to stress not consciousness and human liberty, but instead the unconscious and those factors that condition the human being.

It should be noted that the concept of "structure" and the method inherent to it came to structuralism not directly from the logico-mathematical sciences, or even from psychology (the Gestalt school), all of which had been working with these ideas for some time, but from linguistics. Thus, it has been said that structuralism was born out of an "exorbitation of language,"[40] linguistic concepts applied beyond their field to other disciplines. Indeed, one point of reference common to all the distinct manifestations of structuralism has been the 1915 work *Course in General Linguistics*[41] by the Swiss linguist Ferdinand de Saussure (1857–1913). This work not only made a decisive contribution to the foundation of modern linguistics but also introduced the use of the "structural method" to the study of language.

To this we must add that the roots of structuralism, especially with respect to literary and æsthetic theories, lie in that vast and motley movement known as "formalism," which appeared in Russia during the period of the Revolution and soon came to have wide influence on European art and philosophy in the early twentieth century. Formalism, or more precisely "the formal method," first appeared in the æsthetic theories of the Russian futurists, who proclaimed the necessity of revolutionizing literature and the arts along with society. For the futurists, "[i]n order to recover the sensation of life, art had to *defamiliarize,* to make objects unfamiliar by making forms difficult, shattering the layer of custom on our

40. Anderson, *In the Tracks of Historical Materialism,* 40.
41. Saussure, *Course in General Linguistics.* Hereafter cited as *Course.*

humdrum perceptions; and defamiliarization, in turn, had to be achieved through the constant use of unmotivated formal *devices*...invariably based on *deviation* from established norms of language and style."[42] The futurists privileged the formal aspects of a work of art over the work's content.

It was the Russian linguist Roman Jakobson who performed the important role of bringing together structuralism's diverse historical components and introducing the structuralist interpretative method of linguistics to the other human sciences. In Jakobson there intersect the most varied lines of structuralist development: taking as his point of departure the experience of Russian formalism (whose æsthetic ideas he helped to spread), he developed the ideas of Saussure, first in the Prague Linguistic Circle, of which he was a founder, and later in the United States. It was in New York, where he had fled to escape the war, that Claude Lévi-Strauss, through his friendship with Jakobson, came into contact with linguistic structuralism.

Let us now examine the basic ideas of Ferdinand de Saussure's theory, so that we may see why it had such great importance for the development of structuralism.

For Saussure, language, a faculty common to all people, cannot be conceived of merely as the sum of the speech acts (both past and all possible future) that individuals perform in order to communicate among themselves. The fundamental distinction to be made in linguistics is that which exists between *language* and *speech* (in French, *langue* and *parole*). A language is "a system of signs expressing ideas" (*Course,* 15) and is "the social part of language, external to the individual, who by himself is powerless either to create it or to modify it. It exists only in virtue of a kind of contract ... between the members of a community" (*Course,* 14). Speech, in

42. Shklovsky, "Art as Technique," 12. Also quoted in Merquior, *From Prague to Paris,* 22.

contrast, is a single act of verbal communication performed by an individual in order to express a thought. The first concept, language, refers to the system of rules that underlies every act of speech and that, as the common heritage of the community, exists independently of the subject-user. If an individual were not familiar with this system of rules, which each individual masters through a period of apprenticeship, no act of speech would be possible. Linguistics, for Saussure, is fundamentally the study of *language* (*langue*), and is therefore but a single branch of a more general discipline, a science of signs, *semiology*, which he hopes will be developed in the future.

Saussure also makes a second basic distinction involving a linguistic sign: between the signal or word, the "signifier," and the concept, what is meant or "signified."[43] Early on, Saussure defines the linguistic sign as the union of a "concept" and a "sound image" or "sound pattern" (*image acoustique*), which is "not actually a sound [but] the hearer's psychological impression of a sound, as given to him by the evidence of his senses" (*Course*, 66). Later, in order to avoid possible ambiguity, Saussure proposes to call the concept the "signified" and to call the sound-pattern the "signifier." In both cases, though, the key point that arises out of Saussure's analysis is the following: the link between the two components of a linguistic sign is arbitrary, so that the same concept, the "abstract" concept "sister," for example, may be tied to different sound-patterns in different languages (*sister, soeur, sorella, hermana,* and so on). There is no apparent reason, then, that any given sound-pattern should be associated with any given concept: any other sound-pattern would be equally effective and satisfactory. This does not

43. In French, respectively, *signifiant* and *signifié,* which are here translated using the customary American terms "signifier" and "signified." See note in Bibliography under Saussure. [Trans.]

mean that the speaker may freely modify the association between the two terms; should the individual do so, communication would be seriously, perhaps fatally, compromised.
Rather, the association, while arbitrary, is socially given at a
particular historical moment. It is clear that language
changes over time, but for any given linguistic community
what counts is its present situation, which is what allows
communication between individuals.

And there are further corollaries to this insight. Not only
does a language produce a unique system and range of signifiers, dividing and organizing the acoustical spectrum in a
way that is simultaneously arbitrary and specific; it also does
the same thing with the spectrum of conceptual possibilities
as well: a language possesses a way, a mode, similarly arbitrary and specific, of dividing and organizing the world into
concepts and categories – that is, it has its own way of creating signifieds. This is not hard to see if we recall that not
infrequently there are particular words, expressions, or con-
structions in one language that cannot easily be translated
into another language, and this is precisely because the
signifieds of the two languages in question are not entirely
equivalent – they belong to distinct articulations of the conceptual plane. Thus, signifieds do not exist in and of themselves; they are not fixed entities valid for all languages that
each language simply expresses by means of its own particular signifiers. Signifiers (words) and signifieds (meanings),
precisely because they are the arbitrary divisions of a contin-
uum – conceptual in one case, acoustic in the other – can be
defined only on the basis of relationships, as functions of a
system of reciprocal differences: each one is defined by what
the others of its plane are not.

An example from Saussure himself will make this point
clearer: "We assign identity ... to two trains ('the 8:45 from
Geneva to Paris'), one of which leaves twenty-four hours af-

ter the other. We treat it as 'the same' train, even though probably the locomotive, the carriages, the staff etc. are [different]" (*Course,* 107). What gives identity to the train is its position in the system of trains described by the railway schedule. The important thing is to be able to distinguish it from all other trains *defined in the same way.* Here is the way Saussure explains this key point in his linguistic theory, the "differential conception" of signifieds and signifiers: "The sound of a word is not in itself important, but [rather] the phonetic contrasts which allow us to distinguish that word from any other. That is what carries the meaning" (*Course,* 116). "[C]oncepts ... are purely differential. That is to say they are concepts defined not positively, in terms of their content, but negatively by contrast with other items in the same system. What characterises each most exactly is being whatever the others are not" (*Course,* 115).

One further distinction must yet be considered, and that is one Saussure drew between *synchrony* and *diachrony.* We have all had the experience of finding that language is in constant change. Linguistic signs are not static; they constantly evolve and change. This fact can be immediately verified with respect to signifiers, but it is equally true for signifieds. For example, the English word *silly* meant or signified "pious" or "good" until the sixteenth century, when it began to take on the meaning "innocent" and "helpless." But from there the meaning continued to change, until today, when the same word now means "stupid," "foolish." Saussure observed that one can study the language *diachronically,* in its historical dimension, following the transformations of the linguistic signs through time, or one can study it at a given historical moment, in its *synchronic* dimension. The synchronic aspect is the only one that matters to those who *use* language, Saussure felt, as it is the one that allows the present system of internal relationships, that is, the rules of a language (the *langue*), to be studied and clarified. It is for this reason that Saussure gave primary importance to synchronic analysis in the field of linguistics.

The ideas treated here (in a very summary way) are the most fundamental and innovative of Saussure's *Course in General Linguistics*. We should recall that the *Course* is a reconstruction of Saussure's thought by two of his colleagues from lecture notes taken by his students and published posthumously in 1915. Interestingly, the term *structure* never appears in the *Course,* but rather *system,* which is the term by which, as we have seen, Saussure assigns to language the condition of a unified whole whose parts are interdependent. *Structure* is a word used in a general sense to designate the mode of organization of such a system on the basis of the roles, the ranks, the relationships, and so on, of its parts. And it is in this sense that the word was later used in structural linguistics, appearing for the first time in the Prague Circle, whose members spoke of the "structure of the linguistic system."

From what we have reviewed here it is clear that language, in Saussure's analysis, possesses some singular properties: on the one hand it is composed of completely arbitrary signs, while on the other it presents a rigid, impersonal, external structure that precedes the individual, who can neither create it nor significantly transform it. This structure functions as a kind of social *a priori:* though not consciously perceived, it exerts a fundamental influence on those who learn and use the language in that to a great extent it determines the quality and breadth of the individual's cognitive horizon. People assimilate the language long before they are able to "think for themselves." Indeed, this apprenticeship constitutes the *basis* for what might be called "thinking for themselves." It is true that after some experience with the language and its possibilities people become able to favor some signifieds or meanings and to reject others, but they cannot easily change the system of associations between signifiers and signifieds, between words and meanings, a system that has been socially established and that the language-learning apprenticeship has deposited in the memory of each member of the language community. Put another way, one always thinks from *inside* a language, and the language is an interpretative form of reality. This interpretative form significantly restricts the space within which a subject may consciously construct his or her "own" experience and freely express it through language. From this idea derives the notion that in perception there is not a first "perceiving" moment that can be distinguished from a later moment at which that perception is consciously articulated in language; there would appear to be one single moment of perception-interpretation, awareness of which in large measure eludes the "subject."

These ideas will help us understand the generally anti-subjective and anti-humanist attitude that structuralists arrived at from Saussure's linguistic paradigm. Moreover, the disregarding of diachronic analysis of evolution of language over time and the privileged position accorded to synchronic analysis, which is the method that allows one to recognize structures, turned history into a series of disconnected "vignettes" in which, although the setting and backgrounds might change, human beings were always subject to unconscious conditionings. What follows from this view is a "history without a subject."

Claude Lévi-Strauss (b. 1908), who might be considered the "father" of structuralism, is not a linguist; he is an anthropologist educated in the tradition of French sociology of Emil Durkheim and Marcel Mauss. His contact with Jakobson convinced him that the approach used by linguistic structuralism offered the best tool for delving into sociocultural phenomena – the objects of study for anthropology – with the ultimate aim of finding and precisely defining those *universal constants* of human societies that Durkheim had been searching for. Thus, adopting the methods of linguistic structuralism, Lévi-Strauss proposed that anthropology be reduced to a semiotics – that is, that human cultures be studied as structures of verbal and nonverbal languages.[44]

In its study of a culture, anthropology focuses on a series of systems, such as kinship, marriage rites, food, myths, and so on, each of which is a combination or complex of processes that allows a specific type of communication, and can therefore be treated like a language that operates at one of several levels of social life, each with its own particular system of signs. The structured whole of all these languages constitutes the totality of the culture, which, from this point of view, can be seen as a kind of global language.

Thus, analyzing the complex systems of division into totemic clans in so-called primitive tribes, Lévi-Strauss finds that a form of communication occurs in and through them, finds that they are a "language." To a "modern" observer, these systems can seem absurd, "primitive," in that they appear confused, naive, lacking rationality. But when "primitive" people divide the universe in accordance with the characteristics of their clan, some of which characteristics may also be shared by certain animals, plants, or stars,[45] they are constructing a system of divisions, contrasts, differentiations between themselves and the other members of the tribe, and it is these differentiations that allow the very existence of the tribe itself as an *articulated and not indistinct* whole. They

44. Lévi-Strauss, *Structural Anthropology,* vol. I, chaps. 3 and 4. Hereafter cited as *Struc. Anthro.*
45. For example, a warrior and bird of prey and mountain and star may all come to be associated with a certain quality such as fearlessness or wisdom.

are constructing a system of social communication, which is precisely what keeps the tribe united. This operation is not "primitive" in any way, but is, rather, highly sophisticated, in the sense that the members of the clan are joining things *that are not proximate in perceptual experience,* and this is precisely the essence of all signs and the operation of signifying itself.[46]

In this way, when a person identifies with her totemic animal, that "primitive" person does not perceive herself as an animal, as a naive ethnologist might be led to believe, but rather "interprets" herself as that type of animal; that is, the person transforms herself into a sign for herself *and* for the other members of the tribe, thus entering into the "discourse" of the society.

"Savages" organize their mental world in a way that Lévi-Strauss calls "analogical," since they use the natural objects that surround them to construct their signs in the way a *bricoleur* (handyman) does when creating or repairing something using pieces of objects found at hand. From this point of view, the "savage mind" is different from the modern or "logical" mind, which invents artificial signs and superimposes them onto nature in the way that an engineer does. Nevertheless, the savage mind is no less abstract than the modern mind, and no less distant from the world of pure sensory impressions than is the modern mind. In this regard, the study of the complex systems of kinship in primitive societies is most illuminating. Speaking of these systems, Lévi-Strauss says: "A kinship system does not consist in the objective ties of descent or consanguinity between individuals. It exists only in human consciousness; it is an arbitrary system of representations, not the spontaneous development of a real situation" (*Struc. Anthro.,* 49).

46. See Lévi-Strauss, *The Savage Mind,* Chapter III: "Systems of Transformations," 75–108. Hereafter cited as *Savage Mind.*

For Lévi-Strauss, then, the difference between ourselves, modern human beings, and so-called "primitives" lies not in some distinct mental capacity, but rather in a different sphere of application of the same mental energies. The "savage mind" is exactly the same as the "modern mind," and the functioning of the former is the same as the functioning of the latter: both construct their own realities and project them onto whatever reality they find around them, although in neither case is this operation a conscious one. In summary, what arises is a structuring, *symbolizing* function of the human mind, and it exists at all times, in all places, in all societies, although it may be expressed in different forms.

Nor is the analogical mode of thinking typical of totemism limited only to "primitive" peoples; it may be found everywhere – in sports clubs, for example, where players give their teams the names of animals so as to indicate their own special temperament or some other physical characteristic and thereby distinguish themselves from other clubs. It is simply that we no longer recognize this mentality, or it seems "strange" to us. This strangeness arises when human beings stop interacting analogically *with* nature and are interested only in acting "logically" *upon* it.

Lévi-Strauss is a stern and bitter critic of "modern man" and modern society, which he defines as a "monstrous cataclysm" that threatens to swallow the entire planet. In this regard he anticipates many of the themes of the environmental movements that have appeared since his writings. In his view, what we call "progress" has been possible only at the cost of violence, slavery, colonialism, and the destruction of nature; progress is only an ethnocentric illusion on the part of our civilization, a *myth,* and as such possesses no greater or lesser arbitrariness than, and the same function of "social truth" as the products of the primitive mind.

Indeed, in Lévi-Strauss's view there is no such thing as Progress, because there is no history as the objective succession of events. History is simply a system of signs, by definition unjustified, that are determined by other, non-historical realities. In fact, Lévi-Strauss contends that all expressions of History (that is, the various forms under which history is told), like those of language, totemism, and myths, choose their signifier units out of a pre-existing terminological matrix, which in the case of History is constituted by what we think of as "historical facts." But the selection, organization, and therefore the interpretation of these "historical facts" – in a word, the meanings that are attributed to them – are in Lévi-Strauss's view arbitrary and are determined by a culture's projection onto them of that culture's own current situation. That is, if we take an interest in a particular historical period – the French Revolution, for example – it is because we believe that the French Revolution can offer us an interpretative and behavioral model for the present day. History itself neither gives meanings nor represents progress; it is only a catalog of events, a method, that can be used in a variety of ways.

It is clear that Lévi-Strauss's thought could not avoid a clash with that of Sartre, his perfect antithesis. In his 1960 work *Critique of Dialectical Reason,* Sartre had tried to achieve a synthesis of existentialist humanism and Marxism. For him, history had its own special intelligibility; it was human beings who constructed it. Furthermore, Sartre's philosophy in its humanist aspect tends to show that the meaning, continuity, and purpose attributed to collective human action are intrinsic components of historical comprehension. History therefore cannot be reduced to a merely natural, biological phenomenon.[47]

47. See Soper, *Humanism and Anti-Humanism,* Chap. 5.

The following quotation, from the last chapter of *The Savage Mind* (1962), which is in large part devoted to a refutation of the *Critique of Dialectical Reason*, is Lévi-Strauss's evaluation of Sartre's historicism and humanism:

> We need only recognize that history is a method with no distinct object corresponding to it to reject the equivalence between the notion of history and the notion of humanity which some have tried to foist on us with the unavowed aim of making historicity the last refuge of a transcendental humanism: as if men could regain the illusion of liberty on the plane of the 'we' merely by giving up the 'I's that are too obviously wanting in consistency (*Savage Mind*, 262).

In the thought of Lévi-Strauss, just as there is no such thing as an individual subject (we recall that he defined the "I" of the phenomenological tradition as an *enfant gâté,* a spoiled child), so, too, there is no collective subject, no humanity who creates history and gives a conscious continuity to events. On the basis of the modern idea of historicity, which has been used to smuggle in the idea of human liberty, and with it humanism, Lévi-Strauss finds that we live in a "hot" society – a society that by means of an internal dialectic is constantly generating social change, and therefore constant tensions and conflicts. It is a society that functions like a thermodynamic machine, producing a high degree of order at the cost of an enormous consumption of energy and huge internal imbalances – in other words, a machine that generates entropy: an overall disorder greater than its internal order. In contrast to modern societies, primitive societies are "cool," in that they try to limit change, to avoid history. They do this by maintaining a low standard of living (also thereby producing the desirable side-effect of preserving the environment), trying to control demographic growth, and basing power on consensus (*Struc. Anthro.*, vol. II, chap. 1).

At this point we can clearly see one of the several paradoxes in Lévi-Strauss's thought, one that his many critics have not failed to point out:[48] after Lévi-Strauss handed down such a harsh and negative judgment of industrial society, one would have expected him to repudiate science, or more generally, the "scientific gaze" or world view that objectifies nature, transforms nature into a thing, an object of study, for the development of our "entropic society" has gone hand in hand with advances in science and technology. Surprisingly, however, Lévi-Strauss situates his own research in the realm of the natural sciences; indeed, he frames it within the most rigorous and all-encompassing materialist scientism. Here is the way he declares himself in a famous passage:

> I believe the ultimate goal of the human sciences [has been] not to constitute, but to dissolve man. The pre-eminent value of anthropology is that it represents the first step in a procedure which involves others. Ethnographic analysis tries to arrive at invariants beyond the empirical diversity of human societies.... However, it would not be enough to reabsorb particular humanities into a general one. This first enterprise opens the way for others ... which are incumbent on the exact natural sciences: the reintegration of culture in nature and finally of life within the whole of its physico-chemical conditions (*Savage Mind,* 247).

In an ultimate reduction, Lévi-Strauss contends that the various types of human societies derive merely from various configurations of the structural elements of the human mind, whose roots are to be found in the biochemical and biophysical functioning of the body-brain. For the human mind is no more than an attribute of the human brain and constitutes a *closed system,* like a kaleidoscope in which continual move-

48. See Merquior, *From Prague to Paris,* 68–74.

ments produce an abundance of forms and colors, but always on the basis of a few simple elements.

Clearly, this radical naturalism and anti-humanism lends itself to objections at several levels. The most immediate objections might be to its failure to adequately include the position and role of the observer. After all, it is always a human being studying human-being-ants. As the phenomenologist Mikel Dufrenne has put it, "Whatever the element is in which it moves, a man's thought will always confront the wearisome task of redirecting the thought back to the thinker; no matter what man says, it will always be a man saying it."[49]

In addition, we must consider the key issue of how to evaluate the interpretations of the structures of primitive peoples' cultures when those interpretations are made by a "modern" mind, which for structuralists by definition possesses an unconscious configuration different from those it is attempting to interpret. Lévi-Strauss recognized that his interpretations of primitive myths are a kind of translation of the semantic code of the "savage mind" into a different, "modern" code, and in that sense are themselves necessarily *mythic*. And if this is true, as the post-structuralist philosopher Jacques Derrida has pointed out, it is difficult to understand why they should be taken seriously.

49. Dufrenne, "La philosophie du néo-positivisme," 783.

5.2 Michel Foucault

MICHEL FOUCAULT (1926–1984), whose basic ideas on the human being and whose critique of humanism we will examine shortly, always maintained that he was not a structuralist. In his opinion that label was meaningless because it lumped together figures who really had very little in common.[50] Describing his education and the general climate that prevailed during the period when his thought was being formed, Foucault said he felt himself part of that generation of young people in the early fifties who no longer recognized themselves in the existentialism of Sartre and Merleau-Ponty with its insistence on problems of "meaning." Foucault's generation, coming after Lévi-Strauss's studies of human societies and Lacan's studies of the unconscious, saw the problems addressed by existentialism as superficial and somewhat futile. What really needed to be investigated was "the system." These are the reasons Foucault gave for this: "In all periods, the people's way of thinking, their way of writing, judging, speaking (even in their conversations on the street and in their everyday writing), and even the way people experience things, the reactions of their sensitivity, their whole behavior, is governed by a theoretical structure, a system that changes over time and from society to society but that is present at all times and in all societies."[51]

Thinking is never truly free, Foucault goes on to say; that which is thought always occurs "inside an anonymous, constricting thought which is the thought of a time and a language.... The task of philosophy today...is to bring to light

50. El Kabbach, "Foucault répond à Sartre," 20–23. Hereafter cited as El Kabbach.
51. Chapsal. "Foucault s'affranchir de l'humanisme," 14–15. Hereafter cited as Chapsal.

that thought which is prior to thought...that background against which our 'free' thought emerges and sparkles for an instant" (Chapsal, 33–34).

That is Foucault's definition of the basic aspects of the problem that he was addressing. Thus, the goal of his entire body of work, he says, has been:

> ...to try to find in the history of science, the history of disciplines and of human knowledge, something like its "unconscious." If you wish, the hypothesis of the work is generally this: the history of knowledge does not simply obey the idea of the progress of reason; human consciousness or human reason cannot arrogate to itself the laws of its history. There is something, beneath what science knows of itself, that it does not know, and its history, its change, its episodes, its accidents obey a certain number of laws and determinations. It is precisely those laws and those determinations that I have attempted to bring to light. I have attempted to get to the bottom of an autonomous domain that would be the domain of the unconscious of science, the unconscious of knowledge, which would have its own laws just as the human individual's unconscious also has its laws and its determinations (El Kabbach, 43).

Moreover, Foucault believed that one of the most serious stumbling blocks faced by philosophy today was the idea of "humanism." Therefore, one of the principal tasks of his work was to purge philosophy of such an idea. In his own words, "the discoveries of Lévi-Strauss, Lacan, Dumezil... erase not only the traditional idea that has been held about man, but also, in my view, all tend to make the very idea of man useless for research and for philosophy. The most damaging legacy we have inherited from the nineteenth century, and which it is time we got rid of, is humanism" (Chapsal, 34).

Foucault had been a brilliant student, his formal education being in philosophy and psychology, and he began his career in 1961 with a profoundly original work entitled *Madness and Civilization: A History of Insanity in the Age of Reason*. In this book Foucault writes a history of madness in the West, beginning in the Renaissance and passing through the Age of Reason (the *"âge classique"*) to the nineteenth century, to the foundation of psychiatry as a "science." Foucault inverts the normal, optimistic interpretation or image of psychiatry as a discipline that is in constant evolution and growth; his book is a kind of counterhistory of the discipline. Madness emerges in his study as a concept that shifts through history, assuming different and sometimes contradictory forms and in general depending upon the complex of beliefs that characterizes a given period.

Thus, in the Renaissance, during which "madmen" were often allowed to roam freely, madness somehow seemed to "speak" to the sane from a world that reason did not or could not reach; similarly, in the combination *king-jester* (the fool), madness defies reason by showing the dementia that exists in "rationality" and by bringing rationality face to face with the "reason" that lies in madness. In the succeeding age, the Age of Reason, madness is separated from reason and becomes non-reason: those who are mad are now locked up in jails and asylums, together with the poor, vagabonds, criminals, the unemployed – all those who might constitute a threat to society. The unifying characteristic of this heterogeneous group was that its members' behavior diverged from what the society of the time considered "rational."

Toward the end of the eighteenth century the modern phase began, with the reforms that segregated madmen from their companions in misfortune and gave rise to the "mad

house" *per se* as the locus of confinement and medical treatment. From this point on, the madman becomes an object of
psychiatric study and practice, the object of a body of knowledge that is constituted out of the result of those activities.
Madness is now "mental illness," and it "speaks" in conformity with medical discourse; the madman himself is mute,
while on his behalf many different, mutually conflicting interpretations, incessantly constructed by psychiatrists, are
spoken. In modern society madness, relegated by force to the
madhouse, "cries out" through art – its only locus of expression – and defies and relativizes bourgeois "normality," it
cries out in the voices of de Sade, Hölderlin, Van Gogh,
Nietzsche....

However well received it may have been in academia and
anti-psychiatric circles, Foucault's book had no great general
impact. And much the same happened with his next work,
which was on a similar subject: *The Birth of the Clinic: An
Archæology of Medical Perception.* It was only with the
publication in 1966 of a work titled *Les mots et les choses:
une archéologie des sciences humaines* (in English, in a title
suggested by the author: *The Order of Things: An Archæology of the Human Sciences*) that Foucault found great success even among a non-specialist readership, a success that
catapulted him to center stage in French philosophy.

In *The Order of Things* Foucault proposed a study of the
fundamental cultural codes that have determined the ordering of human experience in the West. For Foucault, as we
have seen, in no historical period is cognitive activity "free,"
rather, it always occurs within certain determined channels,
within certain forms of knowledge that are given be-
forehand, and which are simultaneously anonymous, unconscious, and inescapable. Foucault calls these forms
"epistemes," a word of Platonic origin that is commonly
used in philosophy with the sense of "true knowledge" or

"science." Epistemes constitute "social *a prioris*" that mark out a specific cognitive space within the totality of possible experience and that determine not only the modes of being of what is known within that space but also the criteria by which a "true" discourse is constructed.

An episteme is unavoidable because, as Foucault says, in any ordering of things or concepts, "there is no similitude and no distinction, even for the wholly untrained perception, that is not the result of a precise operation and of the application of a preliminary criterion."[52]

In that context, it clearly makes no sense to ask whether an episteme is true or false or what its rational value is. It is the episteme itself that determines what can be said and the way recognized truths are constructed in any given period. It is the ground or foundation of all discourses, the conceptual grid that allows or excludes the existence of such truths; it is the *not-thought* by means of which knowledge is modeled and articulated.

The study carried out in *The Order of Things* covers almost the same period as that covered in *Madness and Civilization,* the Renaissance through the nineteenth century. Foucault individuates the various epistemes by characterizing the various historical configurations of three "empiricities," three fundamental areas of empirical knowledge: language, economy, and life. He chooses this approach, he says, because human knowledge in its various forms has always concerned itself, in one way or another, with words, material things, and living creatures. *The Order of Things* is not, however, a history in the usual sense of the word, but rather an "archæology," and in particular (as the subtitle says) an "archæology of the human sciences." By these words Foucault understands a study that begins at the present day and brings to light, as in an excavation, what lies

52. Foucault, *The Order of Things,* xx. Hereafter cited as *Order.*

below the contemporary complex of knowledge, the disciplines that we know today as the "human sciences" – psychology, sociology, literary criticism, and historiography, and also the "counter-sciences," as Foucault calls them: ethnology, psychoanalysis, and linguistics. But the purpose of the study is not to reconstruct the history of the development of these disciplines; instead it is to arrive at a diagnosis of their present-day cognitive status – that is, their capabilities, validities, and limits as "sciences of the human being."

Foucault does not discuss the current contents or theories of these disciplines, just as the archæologist has no great interest in the visible surface of the ground that is to be excavated. Foucault's contention is that a diagnosis of their present state is possible only by reconstructing the episteme that constituted the condition of their existence and that has consequently allowed them to appear and be articulated as they have been. Archæology, as a *method,* attempts to isolate the distinct horizontal strata within which the three basic "empiricities" appear with their distinct orderings. Thus it is that through the ways in which language, material goods, and life have been talked about in the West for the last four or five hundred years it is possible to reconstruct the various epistemes. That which has given rise to the human sciences will emerge in this excavation as a specific stratum, distinct from those that lie below and above it. Through the concept of archæology, Foucault shows himself to have learned, at least with regard to history, the lesson of Lévi-Strauss and, above all, Nietzsche: in order to shed light on present times, he consciously initiates his historical research in the *present.* History is simply an archive, and archæology, through a synchronic analysis of "remains," can reveal its discontinuities, the distinct strata of deposits, though it cannot individuate "historical subjects" or explain why or how the passage from one stratum to another has occurred. Foucault, unlike

Lévi-Strauss, does not seek invariant structures, but rather, like the Nietzsche of *On the Genealogy of Morals,* shows the essential fluidity of all social meanings and values, their constant reinterpretation.

Foucault identifies three epistemes in the period he investigates and the two moments that clearly separate them. The first episteme belongs to the Renaissance, which is characterized by *likeness.* For the Renaissance, all beings are involved in a tightly woven fabric of likenesses and correspondences. Each one leads to the next, to which it is linked by invisible threads, subtle analogies. Renaissance thought did not separate or isolate things but rather joined things among themselves, ordered the world through the supreme metaphor of the human body, in which every part is linked in close relationship and harmony. The language of the Renaissance is, for Foucault, the "prose of the world." Its signs are not arbitrary but return one to the very essence of things: between signifier and signified there is necessarily a relationship, some sort of likeness that the scholar may – indeed *must* – discover. Knowledge is, then, fundamentally *interpretation,* the exegesis of the great book of the world that God has written for humankind; it is the quest after "signs," the writing that the hand of God has left, like his signature, on Nature.

Suddenly, however, toward the middle of the seventeenth century, this episteme collapsed. The general character of the new episteme that replaces it is that of *representation,* a word Foucault uses to indicate the abstract rationality that divides and individuates: "The activity of the mind...will... no longer consist in *drawing things together,* in setting out on a quest for everything that might reveal some sort of kinship, attraction, or secretly shared nature within them, but, on the contrary, in *discriminating,* that is, in establishing their identities.... In this sense, discrimination imposes upon comparison the primary and fundamental investigation of difference" (*Order*, 55).

In this period, in all fields things are measured, ordered, tabulated, placed in series, columns, structures. Knowledge is spatialized, and all the "sciences" are sciences of order: they are taxonomies, nomenclatures, classifications, following the model of Linnæus's *Botanica*. In all fields, analogy is replaced by analysis. In language, the nexus of likeness, similitude between signified and signifier, disappears: the relationship between them becomes merely conventional, yet at the same time is understood as clear and unequivocal. Words and things belong to two parallel orders; it is the very nature of human consciousness, as created by God, that allows this transparent relationship between thing and concept of the thing, between thing and word.

In turn, this episteme abruptly disappeared toward the end of the eighteenth century, and it was at this point that the modern world *per se* began. For Foucault, the episteme of the modern age is characterized by *historicity* and by the appearance of "man" as such, *man*. Into the metaphor of the "table," which corresponded to the episteme of the age of reason, time and history unexpectedly erupted. In the study of living organisms, for example, which had previously been set neatly one beside the next in rows of classification, the organisms come to be seen not as adjacent in the abstract space of seriality; instead, they are ordered in a true *temporal succession*. Their proximity speaks now of transformation, evolution, of passages and relationships between identities no longer seen as stable. In language, there is the discovery of the strata of signifieds that history is continually laying down: "the word" is no longer a definite, defined, clear entity that leads one back transparently to a concept or a thing in the world, but is now an ambiguous construction, charged with meanings that have been acquired and lost through time. It is here that philology replaces grammar as the center of interest. In economics, the study of the exchange of goods is relegated to a lower importance and *production* becomes central. In all fields, modern thought recognizes dynamism and transformation. The new ordering of things occurs on the basis of historicity. In addition, Foucault sees all categories of modern thought as fundamentally *anthropological,* and this is the most singular characteristic of the new episteme.

In the modern age, Foucault tells us, "representation" does not disappear, but the introduction of dynamic categories that change with time reduces its importance; representation loses transparency and, being static, is unable to give account of *becoming,* of the flux of time. In addition, there is a loss of faith in a God who has guaranteed that the nature of human consciousness will allow us to enjoy a knowledge of the world that is clear and true. As a consequence, "representation" no longer constitutes a common ground for all fields of knowledge; it is no longer *thought* but rather *one mode of thinking.*

This gives rise to the problem of somehow establishing a foundation for knowledge, and Foucault maintains that it is precisely this task to which all of modern philosophy, from Kant to Husserl, is turned. For Foucault, then, modern philosophy is either *epistemology,* the search for a foundation for knowledge, or a search for "meaning." If in a previous time God and the transparency of representation gave an infinite basis for knowledge, knowledge must now be grounded in a *finite* being: the human being. But this being presents a duality that is impossible to resolve: it is "an individual who lives, speaks, and works in accordance with the laws of an economics, a philology, and a biology, but who also, by a sort of internal torsion and overlapping, has acquired the right, through the interplay of those very laws, to know them and to subject them to total clarification" (*Order*, 310). Or as Foucault summarizes a bit later, the human being is one "whose nature ... is to know nature, and itself, in consequence, as a natural being" (*Order*, 310).

In other words, the human being who emerges after the collapse of the rationalist episteme is a natural and finite being, subject to a whole series of limitations and determinations that the "sciences" of economics, biology, and linguistics record in their laws. Human beings are beings who speak a language that is not the individual's own, in which the words of infinite generations have been deposited as a kind of "sediment," beings who enter a world of production already organized and endowed with its own internal rules, who possess bodies subject to all the chemical and physical laws. They are beings born into an already-organized society, with already-established values, beings whose cognitive processes are subject to a whole series of mechanisms and determinisms, beings marked by an original non-transparency, an unconscious, that is, an "other" within themselves that can never be absorbed into the self, as the new human sciences of psychology, sociology, and psychoanalysis will show.

At the same time, the human being, limited and finite, is not only the object but also the *subject* of this knowledge. Indeed, while it is on the human being that this knowledge must be empirically based, the human being must also, at the same time, itself possess or know the elements that give this research meaning. It is within this circularity, then, that the human sciences and all the philosophy of the modern episteme move.

It is precisely this double role as *object of knowledge* and *subject who knows* – a role Foucault considers in detail in the chapter "Man and His Doubles" in *The Order of Things* – that has created all the antinomies and contradictions of modern philosophy, leading it at last into the cul-de-sac where it now finds itself with no way out. It is time to awaken from this "sleep of Anthropology" says Foucault, paraphrasing Kant and his "sleep of Dogmatism" (*Order,* 340–43); it is time for thought to liberate itself from that type of humanism.

It is in this sense that for Foucault *man* is not born until the beginning of the nineteenth century. Foucault uses the word *man* to designate this intellectualist and circular, self-referential construction, although for anyone thinking on the inside of the modern episteme, *man* is simply man.

This strange figure of *man* could only have been born, Foucault says, alluding to Nietzsche, out of the death, or better said, the murder, of God, whose attributes he has tried, little by little, to absorb. It was that act that also gave rise to the human sciences. These are Foucault's words in recounting the parable of *man,* his appearance and his impending end:

> To invent the human sciences was apparently to make man the object of a possible knowledge. It meant constructing him into an object of knowledge. However, that same nineteenth century hoped, dreamed the great eschatological myth of the age, which was that the knowledge of man thereby produced might liberate man from his estrangements, free him from all the constraints over which he had no control; that man might, thanks to the knowledge that he possessed of himself, become for the first time the master and holder of himself. Said in another way, man became the object of knowledge so that man might become the subject of his own freedom and his own existence.
>
> Well, then, what happened – and in this respect one might say that man was born in the nineteenth century – was that, as these researches into man as the possible object of knowledge progressed ... this much-bruited man, that human nature or that human essence, man *per se,* all that – it was

never discovered, never found. When the phenomena of madness or neurosis, for example, were analyzed, what was discovered was an unconscious...which really had nothing to do with what one might expect of a human essence, of liberty or freedom or human life.... The same thing happened with language.... What has been discovered? Structures...but man in his freedom, in his existence – once again, he has disappeared.

But this disappearance of man at the precise moment the roots of man were being searched for does not mean that the human sciences are going to disappear. I have never said that. What I have said is that the human sciences are now going to develop along a horizon that is no longer limited, closed, defined by humanism. Man disappears in philosophy not so much as an object of knowledge as a subject of freedom and existence, since the man-subject, the man that is the subject of his own consciousness and his own freedom, is at bottom a correlative image of God. The man of the nineteenth century is God incarnated in humanity. What results is a sort of theologization of man, a return of God to the earth, which has transformed the man of the nineteenth century into the theologization of himself.... It was Nietzsche who, in announcing the death of God, announced at the same time this deified man that the nineteenth century could not stop dreaming of. And when Nietzsche announced the arrival of the superman, what he really announced was not the imminent coming of a man who would resemble a God more than a man; what he really announced was the coming of a man who would no longer have any relation to that God whose image he incarnated.[53]

And so, for Foucault, the act that killed God has also heralded the death of his killer: "[S]ince he has killed God, it is he himself who must answer for his own finitude; but since it is in the death of God that he speaks, thinks, and ex-

53. El Kabbach, 40–42.

ists, his murder itself is doomed to die; new gods, the same gods, are already swelling the future Ocean; man will disappear" (*Order,* 385).

If *man* is not a constant of human thought but a recent creation, which has arisen within an episteme particular to European culture, then he shall be canceled, wiped away "like a face drawn in sand at the edge of the sea" (*Order,* 387) when this episteme, like those that have preceded it, finally collapses. At the end of *The Order of Things,* Foucault seems to sense that this moment is not far off, that a kind of earthquake is about to destroy the old ways of thought, opening the door to a new way.

These are Foucault's basic ideas on man and humanism as they appear in the texts we have cited, all of which predate the Paris student revolt of May 1968. After *The Order of Things* – and especially following those key 1968 events in Europe – Foucault's philosophical search orbits ever more closely around Nietzsche and becomes directed toward a genealogy of that web of relations that exist between knowledge and power at various levels and in different sectors of society. While in *The Order of Things* "discursive practices" – the ways words are used – are analyzed without regard to the occasion on which they are used or the subject who is speaking or the listeners or their respective social roles, these aspects, and the related problem of power, become central in Foucault's later writings.

According to Foucault, power is not concentrated in a specific "place" – in the State, for instance, as communists believe; power is, rather, omnipresent. In the various institutions of society power is linked to some specific knowledge by means of which that institution has constituted itself down through history. Power-knowledge employs disciplinary techniques and strategies, constructive as well as repressive, by means of which it reproduces and becomes internalized – that is, is transformed into actions that the individual believes to be free. The "subject" thus becomes a product of domination, an instrument of power. Power, therefore, not only represses, it also molds, trains, constructs: it produces objects, organizational structures, rituals of truth, and "disciplined" individuals. Such disciplinary techniques are common to both the capitalist West and the communist East, and do not disappear when power passes from one class to another, from one political group to another.

Foucault's investigation into power-knowledge, which had actually begun with *Madness and Civilization,* reached its maximum expression in his 1975 *Discipline and Punish: The Birth of the Prison,* a genealogy of penal practices, which moves from prisons *per se* into other sites of "confinement" and discipline constructed by bourgeois society: the school, the factory, the hospital. This is perhaps the most mature and seminal of Foucault's works. At the time of his tragic and untimely death in 1984, Foucault was completing a wide-ranging work, *The History of Sexuality,* conceived as a genealogy of psychoanalysis.

6. Recent Years

BY THE EARLY 1980s the various humanisms we have examined were in disorder. Sartrean existentialism had been unable to channel itself into a political expression of any great effect outside the rather restricted spheres of philosophical study and literary production. Heidegger had rejected all previous formulations of humanism, dismissing each as "just another metaphysics," and called instead for humanity to keep silence and prepare for the "new dawn of Being." Theocentric humanism, despite its efforts to make Christianity look like the true incarnation of Humanism, remained mired in its own self-contradictions. Authors such as William (Wilhelmus) Luijpen tried to make phenomenology, too, into a humanism,[54] even when it was clear that what underlay this enterprise was an interest in opening new horizons to Christian humanism. However, none of these efforts was able to reach maturity in the period from its origin to the 1980s. Regarding Marxist humanism, after several attempts to establish distinct camps of "bourgeois humanism" and "proletarian humanism," the upper reaches of the Communist bureaucratic hierarchy finally adopted the position advocated by Louis Althusser.

Thus, the word *humanism* was used in many ways in many contexts and wound up being confused with a vague position having something to do with a "concern for human life in general," beset by problems of society, technology, and "meaning."

And certainly we must not overlook the work of Viktor Frankl (b. 1905), in the "Third School of Viennese Psychotherapy." Though undertaken in a restricted sphere, Frankl

54. See Luijpen, *Phenomenology and Humanism.*

135

successfully applied the teachings of phenomenology and existentialism in a direction totally different from that which the prior deterministic schools of psychiatry had taken. At that time these schools were experiencing a crisis of scientific foundation insofar as they still continued to cling to their myths of origin.

In *The Unheard Cry for Meaning: Psychotherapy and Humanism* Frankl says:

> Logotherapy in no way invalidates the sound and sober findings of such great pioneers as Freud, Adler, Pavlov, Watson, or Skinner. Within their respective dimensions, each of these schools has its say. But their real significance and value become visible only if we place them within a higher, more inclusive dimension, within the human dimension. Here, to be sure, man can no longer be seen as a being whose basic concern is to satisfy drives and gratify instincts or, for that matter, to reconcile id, ego and superego; nor can the human reality be understood merely as the outcome of conditioning processes or conditioned reflexes. Here man is revealed as a being in search of meaning – a search whose futility seems to account for many of the ills of our age. How then can a psychotherapist who refuses *a priori* to listen to the "unheard cry for meaning" come to grips with the mass neurosis of today?[55]

Later Frankl continues:

> This openness of existence is reflected by its self-transcendence.... The self-transcendent quality of the human reality in turn is reflected in the "intentional" quality of human phenomena, as Franz Brentano and Edmund Husserl term it. Human phenomena refer and point to "intentional objects." Reasons and meaning represent such objects. They are the logos for which the psyche is reaching out. If psychology is

---

55. Frankl, *The Unheard Cry for Meaning: Psychotherapy and Humanism*,
   17. Hereafter cited as Frankl.

to be worthy of its name it has to recognize both halves of this name, the logos as well as the psyche (Frankl, 52–53).

Philosophers such as Martin Buber, educated in the West but with their roots in other cultures, also brought illuminating and refreshing contributions to the debate.

And in practice, humanism also operated in other areas far removed from Western cultural traditions and has been an energizing factor in societies that until recently had remained outside the debate on universal ideas. One of the most interesting cases is that of President Kenneth Kaunda of Zambia, who had set up a strong-man government upon the triumph of the anticolonial revolution in his country. His subsequent passage from a lip-service humanism to the *implementation* of a humanism consistent in actions and effects showed all the characteristics of a true "conversion."[56] Suddenly, in a succession of acts of liberation incomprehensible to the bureaucracy that had formed around him, he abolished the country's only political party, which had kept him in power as dictator; he returned his imprisoned political enemies to freedom; he declared the elections that his people had been demanding for twenty-five long years; he was defeated by popular vote and did in fact step down from power. And all this was done while he contributed substantially to the cause of ethnic and political freedom in South Africa and other countries of the region.

56. "Our revolution is a Humanist revolution. We have decided to wage a struggle against imperialism, neocolonialism, fascism, and racism on the one hand, and hunger, poverty, ignorance, disease, crime, and exploitation of man by man on the other. This is what our revolution is all about. Remember that the most important thing to this nation is Man. Man you, Man me, and Man the other fellow. Everything we say and do revolves around Man. Without him there can be no Zambia, there can be no nation. That is why we believe in Humanism. That is why we say man is the center of all activities." (Kenneth Kaunda, Lusaka, Zambia, 20 November 1980).

By the second half of the 1980s Althusser's Marxist anti-humanism was losing ground. Althusser found himself at a dead end in the development of his original philosophy, and there occurred that unfortunate incident that might well be called his symbolic suicide, perhaps as had earlier taken place with the "metaphysical"[57] madnesses of Nietzsche and Hölderlin.

In the meantime, perestroika was making gigantic strides, taking our breath away not only in the West, as might be expected, but also in the bureaucratic strongholds of the Communist parties, both inside and outside the Soviet Union. The official interpretations of social phenomena and the aspirations of socialist society had undergone drastic changes, and "The Report and Concluding Speech by the General Secretary of the CPSU Central Committee at the Plenary Meeting of the CPSU Central Committee, January 27–28, 1987" stated the following: "Our morality, our way of life, is being tested – in this case, its ability to develop and enrich the values of socialist democracy, social justice, and Humanism....In its revolutionary essence, its daring, and its social-humanist orientation, the work that is under way is the continuation of the great work begun by our Leninist party in October, 1917."[58]

This was not simply a question of paying lip service to humanism. The phenomenon of perestroika, with its climate of participation, direct democracy, and distrust of state monopolies clearly embodied the same humanistic tendency that the "young" Marx had unequivocally subscribed to. At all levels a change in attitude had begun, and the theoretical outlines of a new humanism began to appear. For example, Leonid Frolov's *Man, Science, Humanism: A New Synthesis*

---

57. The phrase is from Karl Jaspers.
58. Mikhail Gorbachev, "Report and Concluding Speech by the General Secretary of the CPSU Central Committee," 92.

shows the broadening of vision taking place among the ideo-logues and scientists of the old USSR just before the emer-gence of perestroika.

By the end of the 1980s various movements had begun to return to the paths from which they had strayed since the momentous events of May 1968. This return began, basi-cally, because many members of the sixties generation, who had been the youthful protagonists of the events of that time, found themselves in the early nineties coming into po-sitions of power at many levels and in many spheres. As they recalled with some nostalgia that "wondrous decade," a new "naturalism" began to emerge in many cultural and political forms. Environmental activism, which had begun in the sev-enties, also grew and matured, a further reflection of these leaders' growing influence.

Since the early 1980s, within the contemporary humanist movement the influence of a new kind of theoretical formu-lation known as New Humanism has taken shape in social, cultural, and political organizations, building on themes stemming from phenomenological methodology and existen-tialist currents but structuring them in a fresh way thanks to perspective provided by the thought of Mario Rodríguez Cobos, who writes under the pen name Silo.

Toward a Universal Humanism

1. New Humanism

AS A CONCISE articulation of significant issues in contemporary humanism and New Humanism we find useful certain writings and lectures by Mario Rodríguez Cobos, Silo. First we will examine the introduction given by Dr. Naomi Otero[59] to a 1986 lecture by Silo, in which she briefly describes elements of his thought on the human phenomenon:

> In approaching the human phenomenon, Silo has observed that before human beings undertake to think about their origins or their destiny or other questions such as these, they already find themselves in a specific set of life circumstances, circumstances they have not chosen. That is, individuals are born immersed in a world that is natural, but also social, where they are beset by physical and mental aggressions, which they register as pain and suffering.[60] And attempting to overcome that pain and suffering, human beings mobilize against those aggressive factors.
>
> Unlike other species, human beings are able to extend their physical possibilities by producing and using instruments or tools, *prostheses* (*pros,* "in front of" and *tithenai,* "to put"). Thus, in taking action against painful factors, hu-

59. The following material is from the introduction by Dr. Naomi Otero to a lecture by Silo entitled "Religiosity in Today's World" ("La religiosidad en el mundo actual"). For a related treatment of these themes see also Silo, *Letters to My Friends,* Letter 4, 39–53.

60. In reference to the lecture by Silo "Regarding What Is Human" ("Sobre lo humano"), which distinguishes between an *understanding* of the human phenomenon in general and one's own immediate *perception* or *register* of the humanity of others.

man beings produce objects and signs that are incorporated into society and are transmitted historically. And, in constant reciprocation and feedback, production organizes society, and society organizes production.

This is not, of course, the social and natural world of insects, where experience is passed on genetically; it is a *social* world that modifies the natural, animal state of the human being. It is into this world that each human being is born – a natural world of which the physical body of the individual is a part, and also a world that is not natural, but rather social and historical. That is, it is a world of production (of objects, of signs) that is uniquely *human,* a human world in which everything produced is given – "charged" with – meaning, intention, purpose. And that intentionality is launched, in the final analysis, toward overcoming pain and suffering.

With their characteristic broadening of the temporal horizon, human beings can defer responses, choose among various alternatives, plan their futures. And it is this freedom that allows human beings to deny or negate themselves, to negate certain aspects of their bodies, to negate themselves utterly in the act of suicide, or to negate others. And it is this same freedom that has enabled some human beings to illegitimately appropriate to themselves the social whole – enabled them, that is, to deny freedom and intentionality to other human beings, thereby reducing those other human beings to prostheses, to instruments of the appropriators' own intentions.

Therein lies the essence of discrimination, with its methodology of physical, economic, racial, religious, and other forms of violence. Those who have reduced the humanity of other human beings have in so doing necessarily caused new pain and suffering, and have reintroduced into the heart of society the age-old struggle against nature, although now against other human beings, reduced to natural objects.

This struggle is not, however, between mechanical forces; nor is it a reflection of nature. It is a struggle between human intentions, and it is precisely this aspect that allows us to

speak of oppressors and oppressed, of the just and the un-
just, of heroes and cowards. This is the only thing that
allows the rescue of personal subjectivity, and it is the only
thing that allows the meaningful practice of social solidarity,
that allows a commitment to the liberation of those who
suffer discrimination, whether they are a majority or a
minority.

At this point we need a new definition for the human being. It is not enough to say: "The human being is the social
animal," because other animals are also social. In the same
way it would be incomplete to define the human being simply as the toolmaker or the possessor of language. In Silo's
thought *human beings are historical beings, whose mode of
social action transforms their own nature.* If we accept that
definition, we must allow that human beings can transform
their own physical constitutions as well, and indeed that is
happening.

Human beings first developed prostheses that were external. Today we are introducing prostheses *into* our bodies.
We are transplanting organs, modifying our brain chemistry,
reproducing in vitro. And we have even begun to modify our
genes.

Recognizing that the existence of every human being occurs in a particular situation, a particular set of life circumstances, and that these circumstances exist in the natural
world (whose most immediate manifestation is the body itself) and at the same time in the social and historical world;
recognizing the conditions of oppression that some human
beings have instituted in the world upon arrogating to themselves the whole of the social order – recognizing this we are
led to a social ethic of freedom,[61] an ethic that is an authentic and valued commitment to struggle not only against the

61. In reference to a talk by Silo on the occasion of the publication of his
book *The Inner Landscape (El Paisaje Interno)* at the Eighth International Book Fair in Buenos Aires on April 10, 1982, published as "En
torno a *El Paisaje Interno*," 45.

conditions that produce pain and suffering in *me* but also against those conditions that produce pain and suffering in *others*. For the oppression of any human beings is oppression of myself as well; their suffering is also mine, and my struggle is against suffering and anyone who causes it.

But it is not enough for the oppressors that they have enchained our bodies. They must go further – take from us all freedom, all meaning – they must rob us of our subjectivity. Ideas and thinking itself are made into objects, "things" by the System; "dangerous" or "suspect" ideas must be isolated, locked up, and destroyed as if they were the germs of infectious diseases. Thus, as human beings we must also reclaim our right to subjectivity: our right to ask ourselves what is the real meaning of our lives, and our right to publicly practice and preach our ideas and our beliefs, whether religious or irreligious. And any pretext that is used to block people's exercise of or inquiry into their subjectivity, or their preaching and development of it, anything that stands in the way of it or postpones it, bears the mark of the oppression illegitimately practiced by the enemies of humanity.

In *Contributions to Thought: The Psychology of the Image and Historiological Discussions,* Silo gives a fuller explanation of the theoretical bases of his thought, but it is in *Letters to My Friends: On Social and Personal Crisis in Today's World* that New Humanism is presented with all the vigor of a manifesto. Of course, the "Humanist Manifesto I," inspired by John Dewey, had been published in 1933 and the "Humanist Manifesto II," influenced by the ideas of Corliss Lamont and signed by Andrei Sakharov among others, had been published in 1974, and so, perhaps as a way of distancing himself from the naturalism of the first and the social-liberalism of the second, Silo calls the foundational document (found in chapter six of *Letters to My Friends*) the "Statement of the Humanist Movement." Here are its opening words:

Humanists are women and men of this century, of this time. They recognize the achievements of humanism throughout history, and find inspiration in the contributions of many cultures, not only those that today occupy center stage. They are also men and women who recognize that this century and this millennium are drawing to a close, and their project is a new world. Humanists feel that their history is very long and that their future will be even longer. As optimists who believe in freedom and social progress, they fix their gaze on the future, while striving to overcome the general crisis of today.

Humanists are internationalists, aspiring to a *universal human nation.* While understanding the world they live in as a single whole, humanists act in their immediate environments. Humanists seek not a uniform world, but a world of multiplicity: diverse in ethnicity, languages, and customs; diverse in local and regional autonomy; diverse in ideas and aspirations; diverse in beliefs, whether atheist or religious; diverse in occupations and in creativity.

Humanists do not want masters; they have no fondness for authority figures or bosses. Nor do they see themselves as representatives or bosses of anyone else. Humanists want neither a centralized state nor a para-state in its place. They want neither armed gangs nor a police state in their place.

But a wall has arisen between humanist aspirations and the realities of today's world. The time has come to tear down that wall. To do this, all humanists of the world must unite.[62]

In a 1994 lecture, "What Do We Understand by Universal Humanism Today" ("¿Qué entendemos hoy por Humanismo Universalista?") Silo makes the important characterization of Humanism as an *attitude and perspective in facing life,* making it clear that it is not a philosophy. The confu-

62. Silo, *Letters to My Friends,* Sixth Letter, "Statement of the Humanist Movement," 69.

sion between its defenders and detractors stems precisely, Silo says, from their mistaken conception or framing of this phenomenon, and he calls for a thorough reexamination of the entire question. He goes on to reject the notion that traditional Western and Renaissance humanism is the exclusive locus of the *humanist attitude,* which can in fact be found in many cultures and many regions of the world. Let us review his remarks on these points:

> First we should explain our interest in these themes, since to overlook this might lead people to think we were motivated simply by historical curiosity or some other sort of cultural triviality. For us, Humanism possesses the compelling merit of being not just part of History but also the project of a future world as well as a tool of action for today.

> We aspire to a humanism that contributes to the improvement of life, and that stands in a common front against discrimination, fanaticism, exploitation, and violence. In a world that is rapidly globalizing – throwing people together as it shrinks ever smaller – we see growing symptoms of the resulting clash of cultures, ethnicities, and regions. Such a world must have a universal humanism, one that is both pluralistic as well as unifying and convergent. A world in which countries, institutions, and human relationships are becoming destructured, fragmented, must have a humanism able to give impulse to the forging of renewed social forces. A world in which the meaning and direction of life have been lost must have a humanism able to create a new atmosphere of reflection, in which the personal is no longer irreconcilably at odds with the social, nor the social irreconcilably opposed to the personal. We seek a creative humanism, not a repetitive humanism...a *new humanism* that will encompass the paradoxes of our age and aspire to resolve them....

> While this humanizing process may begin with what is historically recognizable in the West, increasingly it will in

clude events and cultures in other parts of the world where the *humanist attitude* was present long before such words as "humanism" and "humanist" had even been coined. Among the qualities of this *humanist attitude,* which is a position common to humanists from all cultures, the following characteristics stand out: (1) placement of the human being as the central value and concern; (2) affirmation of the equality of all human beings; (3) recognition of personal and cultural diversity; (4) stressing the development of new knowledge that goes beyond the givens of absolute truth; (5) affirmation of the freedom of ideas and beliefs; and (6) repudiation of all forms of violence.

Silo goes on to review some of the prejudices associated with the word *humanism,* observing that such beliefs arise when people fail to realize that today the word itself has little to do, really, with the humanist attitude outlined above:

In fact, the humanist attitude had begun to take form long before the modern era. We can find it in the themes of the poetry of the wandering goliards and in the schools of the French cathedrals of the twelfth century. But the word *humanista,* which designated a certain type of scholar, did not come into use until 1538 in Italy. On this point, I refer you to the observations of Augusto Campana in his 1946 article "The Origin of the Word 'Humanist.'" What I mean to say by this is that the early humanists would not have recognized themselves by that name, which only came into existence much later. Here I might note that Walter Rüegg tells us that in Germany similar words such as *humanistische,* (humanistic) began to be used in 1784, and that *Humanismus* (Humanism) itself began to spread with the work of Niethammer in 1808. It is not until near the middle of the nineteenth century, then, that the term "humanism" came into use in almost every language. We are speaking, therefore, about a recent word, and thus about phenomena that were surely lived by their protagonists of previous eras quite differently from the ways they have been interpreted in the historiography and cultural histories of the nineteenth century.

Silo then takes up once more the question of humanism in today's world:

> We have said that the existentialist philosophers reopened the debate on the subject of humanism, which was thought to be dead. The starting point of that debate, however, was taking humanism as a *philosophy,* when in fact it had never been a philosophical position but instead an approach, an *attitude* in facing life and the people and things and events of life. If the debate took as a starting point the nineteenth-century description of the phenomenon of humanism, then we can hardly be surprised that thinkers such as Foucault would accuse humanism of being part of that whole nineteenth century philosophical approach. And the discussion may also have been influenced by existentialism's position *vis-à-vis* humanism, which posed the question in philosophical terms.
>
> Viewing all this from the perspective of today, clearly it seems absurd to accept an *interpretation* of a thing as though it were the thing itself, and then, based simply on that interpretation, to go on to attribute certain traits to the thing itself. Althusser, Lévi-Strauss, and numerous structuralists have declared their anti-humanism in their works, just as others have defended humanism as a metaphysics, or at the least as an anthropology....
>
> In fact, however, Renaissance humanism had never, in any instance, been a philosophy – not even in Pico della Mirandola or Marsilio Ficino. The fact that many philosophers shared a common *humanist attitude* at that time does not mean that their common attitude was itself a philosophy. Moreover, if Renaissance humanism displayed an interest in "moral philosophy" as it was called, this concern should be understood as part of a broader series of efforts aimed at

dismantling the manipulation of that field practiced by medieval scholasticism.

From that initial error in the interpretation of humanism – taking humanism to be a philosophy – one can easily arrive at any number of very distinct positions. Thus, authors such as Lamont came to define their humanisms as naturalist and anti-idealist, affirming an anti-supernaturalism, a radical evolutionism, the non-existence of the soul, the self-sufficiency of the human being, free will, an intra-worldly ethic, an extolling of art, and humanitarianism. I believe that people have every right to define their particular views in this way if they so choose, but it strikes me as wholly unwarranted to go beyond that to claim that Western historical and Renaissance humanism had followed the same directions, the same paths. I further believe that the proliferation of "humanisms" in recent years is perfectly legitimate, so long as they present themselves as particular manifestations of humanism, without claiming to stand in some absolute way for all of Humanism in general.

Thus, the entire recent philosophical debate with a historical (and localized Western) humanism has been wrongly conceived, wrongly posed. The debate, in fact, is only just beginning, and henceforth Anti-Humanism will have to justify its objections to Humanism in light of the positions of today's emerging and universal New Humanism. We must recognize, moreover, that so far this entire discussion of humanism has been a bit provincial, and that our treatment of this theme – that humanism was born in a certain place and time, was debated in a certain place and time, and whether it perhaps ought to be exported to the whole world as a model of that place and time – has gone on long enough.

Silo then adds with some irony:

Let us concede, then, that the "copyright," the monopoly on the word *humanism* belongs to one particular geographical area. And we have indeed been talking about a humanism that is Western, European, and to a degree Ciceronian. Since, however, we maintain that humanism was never a philosophy, but rather an approach and an *attitude* toward life, can we not then extend our investigation to other regions of the world, recognizing that this *humanist attitude* manifested itself similarly in other places? If not – if we insist upon interpreting historical humanism as a philosophy and, even more, as an exclusively *Western* philosophy – we not only err, we throw up an insurmountable barrier against opening dialogue with the manifestations of this *humanist attitude* that exist in all the other cultures of the earth. If I insist on this point, it is not simply because of the theoretical consequences such an error has had, but more importantly because of the negative consequences it will have for the immediate and universal practice of a *humanist attitude*.

And what is the legacy of the belief that there is a coherent philosophical humanism? Silo observes that:

Historically in Western humanism there has existed a strong belief that knowledge and the mastery of natural laws would lead to the liberation of humanity. But today, we see that there has been much manipulation of knowledge and of science and technology – that often such knowledge has served as an instrument to further domination. The world has changed, and our experience has grown.

Some have believed that religion has dulled and clouded people's minds and, with a paternalistic attitude, have sought to impose freedom by attacking religion. Today, however, we are witnessing violent religious reactions that show no respect for freedom of conscience. The world has changed, and our experience has grown.

Some have viewed all cultural differences as "divergent," believing it was necessary to make customs and lifestyles follow a single mold. Today we are witnessing violent reactions to that attitude as some cultures still attempt to impose their own values without respect for diversity. The world has changed, and our experience has grown.

And today, in the face of this tragic suppression of reason, in the face of growing symptoms of the neo-irrationalism that appears to be overtaking us, we can still hear the echoes of a primitive rationalism in which many generations were educated. They seem to be saying: We were right in wanting to do away with religions because had we succeeded, today there would not still be religious wars; we were right in trying to wipe out diversity because had we succeeded, today we would not be witnessing renewed clashes between ethnic groups and cultures!

But those primitive rationalists have not managed to impose their own exclusive and monolithic philosophy, or way of life, or culture – and that is what counts.

What counts more than anything else, however, is discourse aimed at resolving the serious conflicts we are seeing emerge today. How much longer will it take for us to realize that there is no one culture whose intellectual or behavioral patterns form a model that all of humanity must follow?

I say these things because perhaps now is the time to reflect with some seriousness on making a change in the world and in ourselves. Of course it is easy to say that other people ought to change – the problem is that the other people also think the same thing, that it is others who should change. Is it not time, then, for us to begin to recognize the humanity of *others,* the diversity of you and I, of *all* of us? I believe that today, more than ever, there is urgent need to change the world, and that such change in the world, if it is to be positive, is indivisibly linked to personal change. After all, my life has meaning if I want to live, and if I am able to choose the conditions of my life, or to struggle to attain the conditions I desire for myself and for life in general.

Living with antagonism between the personal and the social has not thus far yielded very good results. We must discover whether it might not make more sense to bring those two terms – the *personal* and the *social* – into a convergent relationship, a unity. Living with antagonism between cultures clearly has not led us in the right direction. We need to go beyond lip-service recognition of cultural diversity and examine in depth the real possibility of uniting as a *universal human nation.*

Silo then concluded his lecture with these words:

I am not one to pontificate on who is or is not a humanist; I wish only to give my opinion here, with all the limitations that such a personal opinion implies, about Humanism. But were someone to ask me to define the humanist attitude in today's world, I would say in few words that a *humanist is anyone who struggles against discrimination and violence, creating new alternatives that make liberty and freedom of choice a reality for all human beings.*

2. Final Words

In the few years that remain to us until the end of the second millennium in the West, it may be that we are glimpsing the outlines of the first planetary civilization. If that does turn out to be the case, then it is possible that New Humanism will indeed find fertile ground for the growth and spread of its ideas. There can be little doubt, however, that this newly emerging planet-wide civilization will arise in a world beset by conflicts and crises that will have a strong impact on each one of us. And it will be then perhaps that we can truly begin, both as a human organization, as a community, and in our own lives as individuals, to ask ourselves profoundly about the destiny of humanity and the meaning of our own actions. New Humanism is precisely an attempt to give answers to these questions.

Appendix

The Crisis of Traditional Humanism and Remarks on New Humanism

A Talk by Salvatore Puledda
University of Rome, April 16, 1996

Introduction: Various Interpretations of Humanism

I wish to thank the University of Rome and the Humanist Student Forum, which have organized this seminar and invited me to speak on the crisis of traditional humanism and the emerging tendencies or currents of recent years that appear to be shaping a new idea of Humanism.

Humanism, as we know, is a subject of vast scope, and moreover one that does not lend itself well to generalizations. Both for this reason and the brief time available to us on this occasion, I will limit myself to presenting a few central ideas, which will certainly require further development and more rigorous language, but which will in any case serve to illustrate to a first approximation the problems of humanism in today's world.

I will begin by pointing out that at present we find the concept of humanism in a most contradictory and ambiguous state. The meaning of the word *humanism* appears lost today, as with the Tower of Babel, in a confusion of tongues and interpretations. And so, before proceeding we will first need to reconstruct and attempt to understand the various historical manifestations of humanism, or at least those that have been of greatest importance. But we should also note that the focus of an investigation of this kind cannot be confined solely to a specialized or academic discourse, as though we were merely trying to find the solution to some historical curiosity. This is because each "humanism" entails, some more explicitly than others, a definition or image of "human nature" or the "human essence." And through this definition, each humanism affirms things affecting issues that are central to every human being, such as how human beings "are" and how they "should be." In other words: each humanism contains a *normative* aspect, a *project* for human beings to put into practice.

If we analyze this theme in a little more depth we will see that each person has his or her own *image* of what the human being is or should be – an image that may be more or less clear, more or less coherent, or may instead be tacit, or a bit confused. And it is on the basis of this image that we try to follow or to justify certain behaviors, and we avoid others. It is also clear that such images are not individual and personal, but that they originate, so to speak, in the cultural "substratum" in which each of us has been formed. This explains the need for our present attempt at clarifying the concept of humanism.

Renaissance Humanism

Let us now turn to the various interpretations of humanism and the various associated "images" of the human being that have been proposed in recent centuries. The first humanism we will consider is the one that we know as Renaissance humanism. Certainly we are all aware of the Renaissance as a vast and complex cultural phenomenon, which presents highly diverse and on occasion even quite contradictory aspects. Nevertheless, with respect to the image of the human being there are certain characteristic features that appear at the beginning and remain throughout the course of the Renaissance. I would summarize them as follows: (1) exaltation of the dignity and freedom of the human being; (2) recognition of the absence of a stable or definitive "human nature;" in other words, the human being is seen not as possessing an essence that is fixed once and for all but as a free and self-constructed being, an idea expressed with particular clarity in Pico della Mirandola's *Oration on the Dignity of Man*, which can be considered a true and fitting "manifesto" of Renaissance humanism; (3) the conception of the human being as a "great miracle," as an infinite being which, as microcosm, reflects within itself all the properties of the universe or macrocosm. As distinct from the modern vision, such a conception of the human being implies that the universe is not simple inanimate matter but is in its own way a sentient and living organism, a sort of macroanthropos. For we who are immersed in the modern way of thought, in the system of truths commonly accepted today (in the modern episteme as Foucault would say), this way of seeing things is extremely difficult to grasp, despite having been an unquestioned truth for the most important figures of the Renaissance such as Leonardo da Vinci, for example.

By the end of the Renaissance, with the birth of the experimental sciences and the development of rationalist and mechanistic philosophies, the human being came to be interpreted as a purely natural phenomenon. Thus began the decline of humanism as a philosophical vision affirming a central position or uniqueness for the human being in the world of nature. By the nineteenth century, with idealism and positivism, the word humanism had completely lost its Renaissance meaning and, when it is used as in Feuerbach, it is within a rigorous interpretation of the human being as a fully and purely natural being.

Twentieth-Century Humanisms: Marxist, Christian, and Sartrean/Existentialist

In this century people have once again begun to speak, and with increasing frequency, of humanism, and the term has now acquired new meanings. Important philosophical currents have defined themselves as humanist, and people speak of Marxist, Christian, and existentialist humanisms. But though attesting to a renewed interest in humanism, each of these currents of thought gives a radically different interpretation of the term *humanism*. Consequently, in our century we find ourselves in the presence not of a homogeneous, complex, and articulated humanist movement as in the Renaissance, but instead in a situation of contention among various humanisms, with each of the three currents we have mentioned having a distinct understanding of the essence of the human being.

In Marxist humanism, human beings are at once natural beings as understood in Feuerbach, while at the same time possessing a uniqueness that characterizes them as "human," that is, as fundamentally distinct from all other natural beings: this characteristic is *human sociability,* the capacity to form a society. For Marx, it is only in society that human beings, through their labor with others, can ensure the satisfaction of their natural needs (food, housing, clothing, reproduction, and so on), and in so doing transform nature, bringing it ever nearer to themselves, making it ever more human. However, human beings cease to be human for Marx when their natural sociability is denied or negated, as occurs in capitalist society, in which their work as a social fact is appropriated by a minority.

In Christian or theocentric humanism, as developed by Jacques Maritain, the principal exponent of this ideology which emerged in the early part of this century, the human being is conceived and defined fundamentally in terms of its limitations with respect to God – persons are human because they are the children of God, because they are immersed in the Christian story of salvation.

In existentialist humanism, as formulated by Sartre in 1946, human beings have no fixed essence but are fundamentally existence launched toward the world, which they construct through choice. The central characteristic of being *human* is the freedom to choose and to choose how to be, to form projects and to form oneself. One ceases to be human upon rejecting this freedom and adopting the behavior that Sartre calls "bad faith," dishonesty, that is: bowing to codified and accepted behaviors under the routine of given roles and social hierarchies.

Moreover, these various interpretations of the nature or essence of the human being have not remained confined solely to the philosophical realm, but as we know have been launched into the political arena through the creation of political parties that have struggled against each other for power. In this way, the formulation of Christian humanism may be viewed within the general movement of the opening of the Catholic Church to the modern world that began in the last century. This opening was intended to develop an ideological basis for political parties of Christian inspiration, which would seek to contain the growing power of liberal and Marxist parties. Sartre, too, tried to formulate his Existentialism as a humanism in an attempt to open a third way in France between the Christian and Marxist parties.

Amid such confusion and the numerous conflicts between these contrasting images of the human being, the word *humanism* in our own century has become devoid of meaning, has broadly come to mean nothing more than a generic concern for human life, which is subject to problems of many kinds extending even to the threat of global catastrophe.

Heidegger's Critique of Metaphysical Humanism

This situation was lucidly analyzed by Heidegger in the late 1940s in his famous "Letter on Humanism," which was his response to questions from a French philosopher on how it would be possible to restore meaning to the word "humanism," which by then had become subject to many diverse interpretations. Heidegger examines deeply and with great acuity the various traditional humanisms, finding in all of them a common, tacit assumption: all modern and ancient humanisms agree, though without sufficiently specifying or investigating this point, that the human being conforms to Aristotle's age-old definition: that man is the "rational animal." No one doubts the second part of the definition, *animal,* but the term *rational* takes on the variable character of intellect, soul, individuality, spirit, person, and so on according to each particular philosophy. Certainly, Heidegger says, in this manner one may assert various truths regarding the human being, but in all of them the human essence is conceived in the same narrow way: human essence is always thought of *from its animalitas* and not *toward its humanitas,* and the human being thus remains reduced to a natural phenomenon, no different than any other entity and, finally, to a thing, an object, forgetting that human beings are always the "who"s posing the question on the being of entities, posing the questions regarding their own essence. This is a fundamental aspect of Heidegger's thought, and also constitutes a central point in any discourse on humanism, and so we will pursue it a bit more deeply.

This examination will also lead us to focus on another image of the human being, the one that currently prevails in today's world, in which the human being is viewed as a "biochemical machine," which is the image of the human being proposed by science or, more precisely, in current positivist or neo-positivist interpretations of science.

Heidegger notes that when human beings in their daily lives, or in scientific practice, are asked what a certain entity *is,* for example, what a stone is, what a plant is, or what an atom is, they answer by saying: the entity is *this,* or it is *that.* For example, a stone is a mineral, a solid, and so forth. In brief, they answer by giving various predicates, various definitions, but always combined with the word *is,* to explain the entity. People discuss whether a given entity is *this* or *that,* but never inquire into the word *is.* The clarification of *being,* which is the basis of any understanding of the entity, remains completely forgotten. Moreover, not only in biology but throughout all the human sciences, the human being is studied and understood as an entity, an object that is no different than any other natural phenomenon, forgetting that it is the human being who is posing the question about entities, who is asking "What is it?" or "What or who am I?" In short, for Heidegger, there is a fundamental difference between objects in the world (entities) and the human being, an ontological difference that the modern view of the human being increasingly tends to reduce and overlook.

Problems with the Current Conception of the Human Being as a "Biochemical Machine"

We have seen how traditional humanisms have viewed human beings beginning with their animality, that is, as a zoological phenomenon along with "something more." However, in our own time, the era of technology, that "something more" tends to be ignored, to disappear, and the human being definitively takes on the characteristics of a "thing." In becoming reduced to a thing, in a technical sense

the fundamental aspect of the human being then becomes
that of *utility*. The human being is now simply a biochemical
or thermodynamic "machine," that is, the human being is no
longer anything other than a work force – a producer – and a
consumer, of things. In this generalized phenomenon of objectification, of reducing people to "things," there is no possibility whatever of forming a basis for values that are related to anything other than utility. The human being, like
the world in general, loses meaning, and life becomes routine, banal; all direction and meaning disappear from human
existence. For Heidegger, this is the root of the nihilism and
immense destructiveness that we see in today's technological
society.

The image of the human being as a "biochemical machine" is currently the dominant conception of the human
being in the West, and that image is beginning to reach, or
has perhaps already reached the level of being "pre-logical,"
that is, it becomes part of the substratum of thought upon
which all our discourse is built and articulated, the substratum that is neither observed nor studied. This image then belongs to the world of "facts" on which there is *a priori*
agreement, a world that is no longer discussed, a world of
unconscious social truth as Foucault would say. However,
the action or influence of this image of the human being
produces a series of problems, some of them serious.

Environmentalism and the Image of the Human Being

Let us consider one such problem that is related to the
area of the environment, an area we all agree is crucial at
this time. In the view of present-day environmentalist currents, it is the *objectification* of nature, treating nature as a
"thing" and transforming it into a purely economic object,

that lies at the root of the critical environmental problems now threatening our planet with catastrophe. Notwithstanding this, most environmentalists do not hesitate to locate themselves within a purely naturalistic view of the human being. For them the human being is simply one more biochemical machine, subject to the laws of evolution of nature, but a machine that is now malfunctioning – we do not know exactly why – whether for genetic reasons, some sort of intrinsic defect, or due to a series of extrinsic factors in the surroundings, the environment.

Having eliminated through this narrowly naturalistic vision all freedom and intentionality in the human being, there remains no other explanation for this defective human functioning than the rigid determinism of the laws of nature. This view, for those who hold it, leads to a sort of inexplicable despair, to a tragic and negative view of the human being who has now become the "villain," the bad animal who destroys all the other forms of life. Paradoxically, in this vision of the world it is the animal world that ends up being assigned all the qualities of natural goodness and kindness previously attributed to the human being by thinkers such as Rousseau. In this way, the animal world comes to possess those intentional psychological qualities of which the human being has been stripped: what follows is a sort of "Disneylandization" in which the ferocity, the aggression, the intrinsic violence of the natural, animal dimension – to dominate, to eat and to be eaten – are overlooked and attenuated until they are almost made to disappear, because in any case life maintains its balance and is preserved. In this view, the human being plays the part of a dangerous and disequilibrating factor and, as a result, within this paradoxical vision, the eventual disappearance of humankind would not necessarily be seen as something entirely negative.

The Left and the Image of the Human Being

A second case of interest relates to those political currents whose roots lie in the Marxist tradition, or more generally on the left, and that are opposed to neoliberalism in economics, denouncing its inhumanity in the name of the higher human values of equality and solidarity. But in a narrowly materialistic conception of the human being, a vision that claims to be fully scientific as such leftist currents do, how is it possible to establish values, which are, by definition, ascientific? How is it possible for a human being – a biochemical machine that obeys mechanical laws – to construct values? And how can the left object so strenuously to the market laws that neoliberalism presents as a scientific mechanism of natural selection played out in the realm of economic activity? Why the objections to these "scientific" market laws, if in the view of the left the human being is indeed a biochemical machine, which as such must be subject to the laws of natural selection, a natural selection that takes place in its (in this case economic) environment? Neoliberalism, based on a sort of social Darwinism, is therefore, notwithstanding its crudeness, certainly more coherent than the position of the left we have spoken of.

I am not saying all this in order to impart lessons to the left (another term that has become quite vague and confused today), but simply to show that in order to move forward, a coherent position with respect to these two areas, the environment and the economy – a position opposing the destruction of both nature and humankind that is inflicted by neoliberalism – such a position will have to abandon its naturalistic conception of the human being, will have to throw overboard the old conception of the human being as a "biochemical machine" and "rational animal," and will have to develop a *new* image of the human being.

New Expressions Since the 1980s

In recent years, that is since the 1980s, new movements have appeared in both the political and philosophical fields as well as the physical sciences, that once again place the human being as the first priority, that restore a special and central position to the human being in the natural world, and that announce a new conception of humanism.

In the area of politics, it seems to me that perestroika, which was initiated by the Soviet leadership in the 1980s, constitutes an extraordinary occurrence which, viewed from outside, seems almost a "miracle." Dr. Zagladin has spoken of both the positive results and the difficulties and shortcomings of perestroika. But bringing the nuclear arms race to an end and reducing the threat of nuclear catastrophe clearly constitutes a true milestone in the history of the modern world, and for this reason I can say in all sincerity that all of humanity owes a great debt of gratitude to the Soviet leadership of those years for the choices that were made under the guidance of General Secretary Gorbachev.

New Humanism

In the area of philosophy, the most recent entry is New Humanism, which owes its inspiration to the thought of Mario Rodríguez Cobos (Silo). Silo has reformulated the concept of humanism and placed it in a historical perspective that is global, corresponding to the times we now live in, when for the first time in human history we are beginning to see the emergence of a truly planetary society.

Silo affirms that the humanism that arose with such vigor in Europe during the Renaissance, restoring the dignity and centrality of the human being that had been suppressed and devalued throughout the Christian Middle Ages, had already arisen in other cultures as well, in Islam for example, and in India and China. Of course, such humanist expressions were known by different names, under references and parameters that varied from culture to culture. But no less an expression of humanism than that of the Renaissance was implicit at certain times in all these other cultures in the form of a *humanist attitude*, a *human approach to life*. In Silo's conception, then, humanism is not a culturally or geographically delimited phenomenon, a purely European occurrence; humanism has arisen and developed in various parts of the world in many periods of history. And it is precisely this phenomenon that now opens the possibility of developing a unifying, convergent direction for all the different cultures of the world which, on a planet interconnected by mass communications, now find themselves increasingly thrown into contact, often without choice and often accompanied by serious conflicts.

Silo locates the human being in the dimension of freedom. Following the phenomenological tradition, for Silo human consciousness is not simply a reflection or copy of the natural world, whether passive or distorted. Human consciousness is a fundamentally *intentional* activity, a ceaseless activity of interpretation and reconstruction of the social and natural world. Human beings, though they participate in the natural world inasmuch as each possesses a body, are not reducible to a simple natural phenomenon, do not have a fixed and unchanging nature, a definable essence. On the contrary, every human being is a project of transformation of the natural world and of himself or herself.

In Silo's thought, our collective human project is to *humanize the Earth*. This means to eliminate physical pain and mental suffering and, in this way, to eliminate all forms of violence and discrimination that are used to rob human beings of their intentionality and freedom, reducing them to things, to natural objects, to instruments of the intentions of others.

Toward a Universal Humanism

Our planet today is rapidly being unified, with peoples and cultures thrown forcibly together, with the result that their various visions of the world encounter other visions with differing purposes and contrasting values. Then what can we find to serve as the common denominator which, while recognizing diversity, will at the same time make possible a convergence, a uniting of the many peoples, the many cultures, the many religions of the world? How can all people come together to create a truly *universal human nation*? In Silo's formulation this is possible as each culture discovers or rediscovers the humanist periods in its own history, in which their finest productions and actions have been associated with the following characteristics: (1) placement of the human being as the central value and concern; (2) affirmation of the equality of all human beings; (3) recognition of cultural and personal diversity; (4) development of knowledge beyond what has been accepted as "absolute" truth; (5) affirmation of freedom of ideas and beliefs; and (6) repudiation of all forms of violence.

Humanism defined as such an *approach* and *attitude* toward personal and community life is not, then, the legacy of any one culture, it is the common heritage of all the cultures of the Earth. And it is in this sense that such a humanism can be spoken of as a *universal humanism*.

Acknowledgments

Grateful acknowledgment is made for the use of excerpts from the following:

Platonic Theology (Theologia Platonica), book XIV, chap. 3, by Marsilio Ficino, trans. Josephine L. Burroughs, published in *Journal of the History of Ideas*, vol. 5, no. 2, April 1944. © 1944 by Journal of the History of Ideas. Reprinted by permission of the Johns Hopkins University Press. • *On the Dignity of Man* by Giovanni Pico della Mirandola, trans. Charles Glenn Wallis. © 1940 by Charles Glenn Wallis, reprinted by permission of Eleanor Glenn, © 1965 The Bobbs-Merrill Company, Inc. • *A Contribution to the Critique of Political Economy* by Karl Marx, ed. Maurice Dobb, trans. S. W. Ryazanskaya, © Maurice Dobb 1970. Reprinted by permission of International Publishers Co., Inc. • *The German Ideology:* parts I & III, by Karl Marx and Friedrich Engels. Copyright 1947 by International Publishers Co., Inc. Reprinted by permission of International Publishers Co., Inc. • *Chance and Necessity* by Jacques Monod, trans. Austryn Wainhouse. Copyright © 1971 by Alfred A. Knopf., Inc. Reprinted by permission of Alfred A. Knopf, Inc. • *Economic and Philosophic Manuscripts of 1844* by Karl Marx, ed. Dirk J. Struik, trans. Martin Milligan. © 1964 by International Publishers Co., Inc. Reprinted by permission of International Publishers Co., Inc. • "Editor's Introduction" by Joseph O'Malley to *Karl Marx's Critique of Hegel's "Philosophy of Right."* Copyright 1970 by Joseph O'Malley. Published by Cambridge University Press, 1970. Reprinted with the permission of Cambridge University Press. • *Reader in Marxist Philosophy: From the Writings of Marx, Engels, and Lenin,* ed. Howard Selsam and Harry Martel. © 1963 by International Publishers Co., Inc. Reprinted by permission of International Publishers Co., Inc. • "Comments on James Mill, *Élémens d'économie politique*" by Karl Marx, ed. Howard Selsam and Harry Martel, copyright © 1976 Progress Publishers, Moscow, and International Publishers Co., Inc. Reprinted by permission of International Publishers Co., Inc. • *Umanismo di Marx* by Rodolfo Mondolfo. Copyright © 1968 by Rodolfo Mondolfo. Published by G. Einaudi. Reprinted by permission. • *For Marx* by Louis Althusser, trans. Ben Brewster, published by Allen Lane, Penguin Press, 1969. © Librairie François Maspero S.A., 1965. Translation copyright © 1969 B.R. Brewster. Reprinted by permission. • *Existentialism* by Jean-Paul Sartre, trans. Bernard Frechtman. Copyright 1947 by The Philosophical Library, Inc. Reprinted by permission of The Philosophical Library, New York. • *Integral Humanism: Temporal and Spiritual Problems of a New Christendom,* Trans. Joseph W. Evans, New York: Charles Scribner's Sons, 1968. Translation Copyright © 1968 Charles Scribner's Sons. Reprinted by permission. • *Education at the Crossroads* by Jacques Maritain. Copyright 1943 by Yale University Press. Reprinted by permission of Yale University Press. • *De Bergson à Thomas d'Aquin: Essais de Métaphysique et de Morale* by Jacques Maritain. Copyright 1944 by Editions de la Maison Française, Inc. Reprinted by permission. • *Being and Nothingness: An Essay on Phenomenological Ontology* by Jean-Paul Sartre, trans. Hazel E. Barnes. Copyright 1956 by The Philosophical Library, Inc. Reprinted by permission of The Philosophical Library, New York. • "Itinerary of a Thought:

Bibliography

This bibliography includes the works referred to in the text. Works from which excerpts are included are marked in **bold**.

Alberti, Leon Battista. *Della Famiglia* ("On the Family," c1432). Published in *The Albertis of Florence: Leon Battista Alberti's* Della Famiglia. Trans. Guido A. Guarino. Lewisburg, Penn.: Bucknell University Press, 1971.

In this work Alberti denies the ascetic life any value, rejects all pessimistic views of humankind, and accords the highest dignity to human action; even as being able to overcome Fate itself.

———. *The Family in Renaissance Florence.* Trans. Renee Neu Watkins. Columbia: University of South Carolina Press, 1969.

Another translation of *Della Famiglia.*

Althusser, Louis. *For Marx.* Originally published as *Pour Marx* (Paris: Librairie François Maspero, 1965). Trans. Ben Brewster. London: Allen Lane, Penguin Press, 1969.

Interpretation of Marxism as a materialism and anti-humanism.

Anderson, Perry, Ronald Fraser, Quintin Hoare. See Jean-Paul Sartre, "Itinerary of a Thought: Interview with Jean-Paul Sartre."

Anderson, Perry. *In the Tracks of Historical Materialism.* London: Verso, 1983.

Bovillus, Carolus (Charles de Bouelles). "The Wise Man" (*De Sapiente*). See Ernst Cassirer.

In this writing the glorification of humankind reaches perhaps its maximum expression in Renaissance humanism; has been called "the worthy epigraph of the philosophy of humanism."

Campana, Augusto. "The Origin of the Word 'Humanist'." Journal of the Warburg and Courtauld Institutes, 9 (1946): 60–73.

Cassirer, Ernst. *The Individual and the Cosmos in Renaissance Philosophy.* Trans. Mario Domandi. New York: Barnes & Noble, 1963.

Chapsal, Madeleine. See Michel Foucault.

Colletti, L. *Enciclopedia del Novecento,* "Marxismo." Rome: Istituto della Enciclopedia Italiana, 1979.

Regarding different interpretations and underlying ambiguities in the works of Marx.

Copenhaver, Brian P. See *Hermetica.*

Doresse, Jean. *Histoire des religions.* Ed. H. C. Puech, vol. 3. Paris: Gallimard, 1976. Also translated as *L'Ermetismo di origine Egiziana* en *Storia delle religioni.* Ed. H. C. Puech, vol. 8. Rome-Bari: Laterza, 1977.

Dufrenne, Mikel. "La philosophie du néo-positivisme." *Esprit: Revue internationale,* 35, 360 (May 1967): 783–94.

El Kabbach, Jean-Pierre. See Michel Foucault.

Engels, Friedrich. *Anti-Dühring* (1878). Ed. C.P. Dutt. Trans. Emile Burns. New York: International Publishers, 1966.

Ficino, Marsilio. *Platonic Theology* (*Theologia Platonica,* 1482), bk. 14, chap. 3. Trans. Josephine L. Burroughs. *Journal of the History of Ideas* 5, no. 2 (April 1944): 22–42.

Foucault, Michel. *The Birth of the Clinic: An Archæology of Medical Perception.* Originally published as *Naissance de la clinique* (Paris: Presses Universitaires de France, 1963). Trans. A. M. Sheridan Smith. New York: Pantheon Books, 1973.

———. *Discipline and Punish: The Birth of the Prison.* Originally published as *Surveiller et punir: Naissance de la prison* (Paris: Gallimard, 1975). Trans. Ann Sheridan. New York: Vintage Books, 1979.

———. *The History of Sexuality.* Originally published as *Histoire de la sexualité* (Paris: Gallimard, 1984). Trans. Robert Hurley. New York: Pantheon Books, 1986.

———. "Foucault répond à Sartre." Interview with Michel Foucault by Jean-Pierre El Kabbach. *La Quinzaine littéraire.* no. 36 (March 1968). Also in *Michel Foucault. Dits et écrits, 1954–1988.* Paris: Gallimard, 1994, 662–668. Also translated as *Michel Foucault: Saber y verdad.* Madrid: Las Ediciones de la Piqueta, 1985, 40–43.

———. "Foucault s'affranchir de l'humanisme." Interview with Michel Foucault by Madeleine Chapsal. *La Quinzaine littéraire,* no. 5 (May 1966), 14–15. Also in *Michel Foucault. Dits et écrits, 1954–1988.* Paris: Gallimard, 1994, 513–518. Also translated as *Michel Foucault: Saber y verdad.* Madrid: Las Ediciones de la Piqueta, 1985, 33–34.

———. *Madness and Civilization: A History of Insanity in the Age of Reason.* Originally published as *Folie et déraison: Histoire de la folie à l'âge classique* (Paris: Plon, 1961). Trans. Richard Howard. New York: Random House, Pantheon Books, 1965; Reprint, New York: Vintage Books, 1988.
Trans. note: This English version is the translation of the edition abridged by Foucault and published in the Plon 10/18 series, with additional material from the original edition including the chapter titled "Passion and Delirium."

———. *The Order of Things: An Archæology of the Human Sciences.* Originally published as *Les mots et les choses: une archéologie des sciences humaines* (Paris: Gallimard, 1966). Trans. Ann Sheridan. New York: Random House, 1970; Reprint, New York: Vintage Books, 1994.

Frankl, Viktor E. *The Unheard Cry for Meaning: Psychotherapy and Humanism.* New York: Simon & Schuster, 1978.
Trans. note: Frankl footnotes the term "intentional objects" as from Herbert Spiegelberg. *The Phenomenological Movement,* vol. 2 (1960): 721, and others have also used it.

Frolov, Leonid. *Man, Science, Humanism: A New Synthesis.* Moscow: Progress Publishers, 1986.

Gorbachev, Mikhail. "The Report and Concluding Speech by the General Secretary of the CPSU Central Committee at the Plenary Meeting of the CPSU Central Committee, January 27–28, 1987." Moscow: Novosti Press Agency Publishing House, 1987. Also translated as Mikhail Gorbachev, *Una revolución en la URSS.* Buenos Aires: Anteo, 1987, 151.

Hegel, Georg Wilhelm Friedrich. *Phenomenology of Spirit (Phänomenologie des Geistes,* 1807). Trans. A.V. Miller, foreword by J.N. Findlay. Oxford: Clarendon Press, 1977.

Heidegger, Martin. *Being and Time.* Originally published as *Sein und Zeit* (Halle: Neimeyer, 1927). Trans. John Macquarrie and Edward Robinson. New York: Harper & Row, 1962.
Trans. note: The passage at footnote 35 is not a standard translation of Plato but rather the English translation of Heidegger's idiosyncratic translation of Plato.

———. "Letter on Humanism." Originally published as *Brief über den "Humanismus"* (Bern: A. Francke Verlag, 1947). Trans. Frank A. Capuzzi with J. Glenn Gray. In *Martin Heidegger: Basic Writings from "Being and Time" (1927) to "The Task of Thinking" (1964).* Ed. David Farrell Krell. San Francisco: Harper & Row, 1977.

———. "What is Metaphysics?" (*Was is Metaphysik?,* 1929). In *Martin Heidegger: Basic Writings from "Being and Time" (1927) to "The Task of Thinking" (1964).* Ed. David Farrell Krell. San Francisco: Harper & Row, 1977.

Hermetica: The Greek Corpus Hermeticum and the Latin Asclepius. Trans. Brian P. Copenhaver. New York: Cambridge University Press, 1992.

Kelsen, Hans. *The Political Theory of Bolshevism, A Critical Analysis.* Berkeley: University of California Press, 1948.

Kelsen, Hans. *Sozialismus und Staat: eine Untersuchung der politischen Theorie des Marxismus.* Leipzig: C.L. Hirschfeld, 1923.

Kristeller, Paul Oskar. *Renaissance Thought and Its Sources.* New York: Columbia University Press, 1979.

———. *Renaissance Thought: The Classic, Scholastic, and Humanistic Strains.* New York: Harper Torchbooks, 1961.
Regarding the origin of the word *humanism.*

Lamont, Corliss. *The Philosophy of Humanism.* 7th ed. New York: F. Ungar Publishing Co., 1990.

Lemon, L.T. and J.J. Rice. See Victor Shklovsky.

Lévi-Strauss, Claude. *Structural Anthropology (Anthropologie Structurale,* 1958). Trans. Claire Jacobson and Brooke Grundfest Schoepf. Garden City, N.Y.: Anchor Books, 1963.
Especially Chapters III and IV: "Systems of Transformations."

———. *The Savage Mind.* (*La Pensée Sauvage,* 1962). [No translator given.] London: Weidenfeld and Nicholson Ltd. Chicago: University of Chicago Press, 1966.

Lothar of Segni (Pope Innocent III). "On the Misery of the Human Condition" (*De miseria condicionis humanæ*). See Jane E. Sayers, *Innocent III: Leader of Europe, 1198–1216*. London: Longman Publishing Group, 1994. See also Sidney R. Packard, *Europe and the Church Under Innocent III*. New York: Henry Holt, 1927.

A work considered highly representative of the medieval mentality, which emphasizes the weakness of the human being and the wretchedness and degradation of human nature.

Trans. note: In light of the vagaries of spelling of the time, the Latin "from the dictionary" and non-exclusively masculine *De miseria condicionis humanæ* and the spelling "Lothar" for the author's name are used.

Luijpen, William (Wilhelmus) A. *Phenomenology and Humanism, A Primer in Existential Phenomenology*. Pittsburgh: Duquesne University Press, 1966.

Manetti, Gianozzo. *On the Dignity of Man*. In *Two Views Of Man: Pope Innocent III On the Misery of Man. Giannozzo Manetti On the Dignity of Man*. Trans. and with introd. by Bernard Murchland. Milestones of Thought Series. New York: F. Ungar Pub. Co., 1966.

———. *On the Dignity of Man*. In *Renaissance Philosophy*, Vol. I, *The Italian Philosophers, Selected Readings from Petrarch to Bruno*. Ed. and trans. Arturo B. Fallico and Herman Shapiro. New York: Modern Library, 1967.

Another translation of *On the Dignity of Man*. In opposition to the medieval view of the wretchedness and degradation of human nature and the weakness of the human body, Manetti's writing exemplifies the new spirit of Renaissance humanism, exalting the whole of the human physical and moral being.

Marcuse, Herbert. *Soviet Marxism*. New York: Columbia University Press, 1958.

Discusses distortions in Soviet Marxism.

Maritain, Jacques. *De Bergson à Thomas d'Aquin: Essais de métaphysique et de morale*. Paris: P. Hartmann, 1944. New York: Editions de la Maison Française, 1944.

———. *Education at the Crossroads*. Originally published as *L'Education a la croisée des chemins* (Paris: Egloff, 1947). New Haven: Yale Univ. Press, 1943.

———. *Integral Humanism: Temporal and Spiritual Problems of a New Christendom*. Originally published as *Humanisme Intègral: Problèmes temporels et spirituels d'une nouvelle chrétienté* (Paris: Aubier, 1936). Trans. Joseph W. Evans. New York: Charles Scribner's Sons, 1968.

Examines the evolution of modern thought and the tragedy of "anthropocentric humanism," which the author asserts was initiated by Renaissance humanism.

Marx, Karl. *Capital: A Critique of Political Economy* (*Das Kapital*, 1867). Ed. Friedrich Engels. Trans. S. Moore and E. Aveling. New York: International Publishers, 1967.

———. "Comments on James Mill, *Élémens d'économie politique*." In *Karl Marx and Frederick Engels, Collected Works*. Trans. Richard Dixon et al, vol. 3. Moscow: Progress Publishers; New York: International Publishers, 1976. Also in Marx & Engels, *Gesamtausgabe*, Abt. 1, bd. 3, 1932. Also in Marx, *Critique of Hegel's "Philosophy of Right,"* xliii. The latter is a different (and somewhat more turgid) translation. [Trans. note regarding footnote 20.]

———. *A Contribution to the Critique of Political Economy*. (*Zur Kritik der politischen Ökonomie*, 1859). Trans. S. W. Ryazanskaya. New York: International Publishers, 1970.
Marx's preface contains a description of his fundamental concept of historical materialism.

———. *Critique of Hegel's "Philosophy of Right."* (*Zur Kritik der Hegelschen Rechtsphilosophie*, c1843–46). Ed. Joseph O'Malley; trans. Annette Jolin and Joseph O'Malley. Cambridge: Cambridge University Press, 1970.

———. *Economic and Philosophic Manuscripts of 1844*. (*Ökonomisch-philosophische Manuskripte aus dem Jahre 1844*). Ed. Dirk J. Struik; trans. Martin Milligan. New York: International Publishers, 1964.
Early works of Marx significant in interpretations of Marxism as a humanism.

———. *Marx's Grundrisse* (*Grundrisse der Kritik der politischen Ökonomie*). [No translator given.] Ed. David McLellan. London: Macmillan, 1971.

———. *Theories of Surplus Value* (*Theorien uber den Mehrwert*). Trans. G. A. Bonner and Emile Burns. New York: International Publishers, 1952.

———. "Theses on Feuerbach," Theses III, VI, VIII and XI in *Reader in Marxist Philosophy: From the Writings of Marx, Engels, and Lenin*. Ed. Howard Selsam and Harry Martel. New York: International Publishers, 1963. Also in *Karl Marx and Freidrich Engels, Collected Works*.

Marx, Karl, and Friedrich Engels. *The German Ideology*, pts. I & III. (*Die Deutsche Ideologie*, 1845–46). Ed. by R. Pascal. New York: International Publishers, 1947.

Merquior, J. G. *From Prague to Paris: A Critique of Structuralist and Post-structuralist Thought*. London: Verso, 1986.

Mondolfo, Rodolfo. *Umanismo di Marx*. Torino: G. Einaudi, 1968.

Monod, Jacques. *Chance and Necessity* (*Le hazard et la nécessité*). Trans. Austryn Wainhouse. New York: Knopf, 1971.
Contains a critique of Engels' scientific ideas as "animistic projections."

Nietzsche, Friedrich. *On the Genealogy of Morals* (*Zur Genealogie der Moral*, 1887). Trans. Walter Kaufmann and R.J. Hollingdale. New York, Vintage Books, 1967.
Evokes the essential fluidity of all social meanings and values, their constant reinterpretation over time.

Packard, Sidney R. See Lothar of Segni (Pope Innocent III).

Pico della Mirandola, Giovanni. *On the Dignity of Man.* (*Oratio de hominis dignitate,* 1486). Trans. Charles Glenn Wallis. Library of Liberal Arts. Indianapolis: Bobbs-Merrill, 1965.
Considered a true "humanist manifesto" of the Renaissance.

Pope Innocent III. See Lothar of Segni.

Pope Leo XIII. *Rerum Novarum* (1891) and *Æterni Patris* (1879). In *Five Great Encyclicals: Labor, Education, Marriage, Reconstructing the Social Order, Atheistic Communism.* New York: The Paulist Press, 1939.
Rerum Novarum adopted a social doctrine to counter the spread of liberalism and socialism. *Æterni Patris* declared the thought of Saint Thomas Aquinas to be the theology best-suited to the Christian world view.

Ruggiero, Guido de. *Storia della Filosofia. Rinascimento, Riforma e Controriforma.* Rome-Bari: Laterza, 1977.

Sartre, Jean-Paul. **Being and Nothingness: An Essay on Phenomenological Ontology.** Originally published as *L'Être et le néant: Essai d'ontologie phénoménologique* (Paris: Gallimard, 1943). Trans. Hazel E. Barnes. New York: Philosophical Library, 1956; New York: Washington Square Press, 1966.

————. *Critique of Dialectical Reason, Theory of Practical Ensembles* Originally published as *Critique de la raison dialectique, précédé de Question de méthode* (Paris: Gallimard, 1960). Ed. Jonathan Ree. Trans. Alan Sheridan-Smith. London: Humanities Press, 1976.

————. *The Emotions, Outline of a Theory* (*Esquisse d'une théorie des émotions,* 1939). Trans. by Bernard Frechtman. New York: Wisdom Library, 1948; Secaucus, N.J.: Citadel Press, 1971.

————. *Existentialism.* Originally published as *L'Existentialisme est un humanisme* (Paris: Nagel, 1946). Trans. Bernard Frechtman. New York: Philosophical Library, 1947.

————. *L'Existentialisme est un humanisme.* Paris: Nagel, 1970.

————. *Imagination: A Psychological Critique* (*L'Imagination,* 1936). Trans. Forrest Williams. Ann Arbor: University of Michigan Press, 1962.

————. "Itinerary of a Thought: Interview with Jean-Paul Sartre" with Perry Anderson, Ronald Fraser, and Quintin Hoare. *New Left Review,* no. 58 (November-December 1969).

————. *Nausea* (*La Nausée,* 1938). Trans. Lloyd Alexander. New York: New Directions, 1969.

————. *The Psychology of Imagination* (*L'Imaginaire: Psychologie phénoménologique de l'imagination,* 1940). Trans. Bernard Frechtman. New York: Washington Square Press, 1966.

————. *The Wall* (*Le Mur,* 1939). Trans. Lloyd Alexander. New York: New Directions, 1975.

————. Philippe Gavi, and Pierre Victor. *On a raison de se révolter: Discusions.* Paris: Gallimard, 1974.

Saussure, Ferdinand de. *Course in General Linguistics*. Originally published as *Cours de linguistique générale* (Paris: Editions Payot, 1915). This translation first published (London: G. Dickworth, 1983). Ed. Charles Bally and Albert Sechehaye with Albert Riedlinger. Trans. Roy Harris. Reprint, La Salle, Ill.: Open Court, 1986.
Foundational work in the field of linguistics. Of the two major English translations of Saussure, the earlier, American version by Wade Baskin (New York: Philosophical Library, 1959) translates *signifiant* and *signifié* as "signifier" and "signified," and those terms are now in general use in the United States. The more recent, annotated English translation by Roy Harris (London: Duckworth, 1983; La Salle, Ill.: Open Court, 1986) uses "signal" and "signification" instead. Because the latter terms do not appear to have the same currency, while Harris's translation is used for quotations of longer passages, the customary American terms "signifier" and "signified" are used for *signifiant* and *signifié*. [Trans. note regarding footnote 43.]

———. *Course in General Linguistics*. Originally published as *Cours de linguistique générale* (Paris: Editions Payot, 1915). Trans. Wade Baskin. New York: Philosophical Library, 1959.

Sayers, Jane E. See Lothar of Segni (Pope Innocent III).

Selsam, Howard, and Harry Martel. See Karl Marx, *Reader in Marxist Philosophy*.

Shklovsky, Victor. "Art as Technique." In L. T. Lemon and J. J. Rice. *Russian Formalist Criticism: Four Essays*. Lincoln: University of Nebraska Press, 1965.

Silo. *Contributions to Thought: The Psychology of the Image and Historiological Discussions*. In *Contribuciones al pensamiento: Sicología de la imagen y Discusiones historiológicas* (Buenos Aires: Planeta, 1991). Spanish in *Silo: Obras Completas*, Vol. I. San Diego: Latitude Press, 1993. English edition forthcoming from Latitude Press.

———. "En torno a *El Paisaje Interno*." Originally published as "Regarding *The Inner Landscape*" (Madrid: Ediciones del Centro de Investigaciones Literarias, 1983). English edition in *Silo Speaks* forthcoming from Latitude Press.
A lecture by Silo on the occasion of the publication of his book *The Inner Landscape* (*El Paisaje Interno*) at the Eighth International Book Fair in Buenos Aires on April 10, 1982.

———. *The Internal Landscape*. Originally published as *El Paisaje Interno* (Madrid: Bruguera, 1982). Trans. Paul Tooby. New York: Community Publications, 1982.
In the trilogy *Humanize the Earth: The Inner Look, The Inner Landscape, The Human Landscape* (*Humanizar la tierra: La mirada interna, El paisaje interno, El paisaje humano*). Spanish in *Silo: Obras Completas*, Vol. I. San Diego: Latitude Press, 1993. English edition forthcoming from Latitude Press.

Silo. *Letters to My Friends: On Social and Personal Crisis in Today's World.* Originally published as *Cartas a mis amigos: Sobre la crisis social y personal en el momento actual* (Santiago: Virtual Ediciones, 1994). Trans. Paul Tooby. San Diego: Latitude Press, 1994.

———. **"Regarding *The Inner Landscape.*"** Originally published as "En torno a *El Paisaje Interno*" (Madrid: Ediciones del Centro de Investigaciones Literarias, 1983). English edition in *Silo Speaks* forthcoming from Latitude Press.

———. "Regarding What Is Human." Originally published as "Acerca de lo humano" (Buenos Aires: Edicil, 1983). English edition in *Silo Speaks* forthcoming from Latitude Press.
Text of a lecture given in Buenos Aires on May 1, 1983.

———. "Religiosity in Today's World." Originally published as "La religiosidad en el mundo actual" (Buenos Aires: Edicil, 1986). English edition in *Silo Speaks* forthcoming from Latitude Press.
Text of a lecture given at Casa Suiza, Buenos Aires on June 6, 1986.

———. *Silo: Obras Completas,* Vol. I. *Humanizar la tierra: La mirada interna, El paisaje interno, El paisaje humano; Experiencias guiadas; Contribuciones al pensamiento; Mitos raices universales; El día del león alado; Cartas a mis amigos.* San Diego: Latitude Press, 1993.

———. **"What Do We Understand by Universal Humanism Today?"** Originally published as "¿Qué entendemos hoy por Humanismo Universalista?" in *Anuario 1994* by the World Center for Humanist Studies (Santiago: Virtual Ediciones, 1995). English edition in *Silo Speaks* forthcoming from Latitude Press.

Soper, Kate. *Humanism and Anti-Humanism.* New York: Hutchinson Publishing Group, 1986.
See especially Chapter 5.

Spiegelberg, Herbert. *The Phenomenological Movement.* vol. 2 (1960):-721.

Stalin, Joseph. *Dialectical and Historical Materialism (O dialektícheskom i istorícheskom materíalizme).* No translator given. New York: International Publishers, 1940.

Thévenaz, Pierre. *What Is Phenomenology? And Other Essays.* Originally published as *De Husserl à Merleau-Ponty. Qu'est-ce que la phénoménologie?* (Neuchatel: Editions de la Baconniere, 1966). Ed. James M. Edie; trans. James M. Edie, Charles Courtney, and Paul Brockelman. London: Merlin Press; Chicago: Quadrangle Books, 1962.

Valla, Lorenzo. "On Pleasure" (*De voluptate,* c1430). Trans. A. Kent Hieatt and Maristella Lorch. New York: Abaris Books, 1977.

World Center for Humanist Studies. *Anuario 1994* (*Yearbook 1994*). Santiago: Virtual Ediciones, 1995.

Yates, Frances A. *Giordano Bruno and the Hermetic Tradition,* chaps. 1–4. Chicago: University of Chicago Press, 1964.

Index

Adler, Alfred 136
Æterni Patris (1879) of Pope Leo
  XIII, affirming Thomism as most
  suitable theology 63
Alberti, Leon Battista (1404–1472)
  13-14
alienation 43, 51-52, 58, 59, 75
  goal of Marxism to eliminate 27
  important in Western Marxism (*see*
    under Marxism) 43
Althusser, Louis 56-57
  adoption of his views by Communist
    bureaucracies 135
  For Marx 56-57
  his Marxist anti-humanism loses
    ground in 1980s 138
  his symbolic suicide as metaphysical
    madness 138
  leading interpreter of Marx's thought
    as scientific 55, 57
  structuralism and 106
Anderson, Perry 107
anguish - *see* Sartre, existentialist
  humanism, and Heidegger
anthropocentric humanism - *see*
  Christian humanism under
  humanism
anti-humanism
  debate just beginning with New
    Humanism 149
  having to justify its positions in light
    of emerging New Humanism 149
  Marxism as necessarily an anti-
    humanism, for Althusser 57
  philosophical 106-134
  philosophical, and structuralism 113
  schizophrenia of modern world and
    coexisting human and inhuman
    values 69
Aquinas, Saint Thomas 63, *see also*
  Thomism and Christian humanism
Aristotle
  Hegel's novel logic and 37

Heidegger's thought and 96, 100
Saint Thomas Aquinas and 63
astrology
  human freedom in Renaissance and 23
atheism
  eighteenth century *philosophes* discard
    idea of God 78
  Sartre's attempt to deduce
    consequences of a coherent atheism
    82
  swift spread in twentieth century as
    threat to survival of Church 61
St. Augustine 16

bad faith
  consciousness' inauthentic fleeing of
    anguish, for Sartre 73
  inauthenticity or dishonesty as
    Sartrean terms, *see* footnote p. 81
Barthes, Roland 106
Being and Time - *see* Martin
  Heidegger
Bloch, Ernst 27
bourgeois society
  based on private property and
    dominance of capital 32
  hypocrisy in 59
  Marx's scientific analysis of capitalism
    and 35
  Marxism as critique of 43, 58
  proletariat and 32
  proletariat siding with national
    bourgeoises during WW I 36
Bovillus, Carolus (Charles de
  Bouelles) (1479–1567) 20-21
  De Sapiente (*The Wise Man*) 20
  his work as "worthy epigraph of the
    philosophy of humanism" 21
  human being as containing all degrees
    of existence 20
  human being as without fixed nature
    20
  ideal of "superior man" formed
    through choice and struggle 20

177

New Humanism Series
Books to Build a Human World

The challenge of building a human world is becoming more vital each day. With every area of existence undergoing rapid change in directions difficult to foresee, no single genre encompasses the breadth of current issues, and the New Humanism Series includes nonfiction and fiction with the unifying thread that each title addresses some facet of the urgent need to humanize both individual and social life, to build a human world.

How can we resolve and develop our personal lives? How can we identify and affect the connections between what happens in society at large and to each of us personally? How can we bring all people together to create a "converging diversity" of genuine cooperation that will be necessary to transform each of us and society as a whole?

With titles by authors from many countries, these books bring you international perspectives that are demonstrating a universal and timely appeal in our increasingly connected planet.

The aspiration for a human world is being put into practice by growing numbers of people in over fifty countries who are volunteering in numerous projects inspired by New Humanism and the Humanist Movement. Latitude Press supports these new cultural activities, the "2000 Without Wars" campaign, neighborhood building activities, and the new vitality reflected in a diversity of other projects. We are committed to publishing these important works, and apply all net income from them to efforts to build a human and nonviolent society.

Below is the list of New Humanism Series titles available as of this printing and forthcoming. New titles are always being added, and you can contact us for current offerings (contact information is on the last page).

Letters to My Friends: On Social and
Personal Crisis in Today's World by Silo

A lucid outline of the "big picture" that makes comprehensible the confusing paradoxes of our time and has led Mikhail Gorbachev to comment: "I recommend this work...Silo and I share very similar views on the current crisis facing both society and the individual."

In ten provocative letters Silo masterfully articulates the approach of a new and universal Humanism – libertarian, pluralistic, and engaged – to the central questions of our time. With keen irony the author strips away the conventional wisdom, revealing that the "emperor's new clothes" of today's unprincipled pragmatism and speculative capitalism are indeed no more than that, a hollow shell of decaying myths that can no longer conceal the horrendous workings of an inhuman social and economic system long overdue for honest criticism and profound transformation. Combines a comprehensive description of current events with specific approaches readers can follow emphasizing local actions.

Current Affairs/Ethics/Humanism   *160 pgs, 5 .5 X 8.25*
$11.95 Softcover   *ISBN 1-878977-23-7*

On Being Human: Interpretations of Humanism
from the Renaissance to the Present
by Salvatore Puledda, foreword by Mikhail Gorbachev

Who are we, these fascinating and restless creatures called human beings? Is there a fixed "human nature" predetermining our actions, or does human existence encompass the liberty to make moral choices, to change the direction of our lives and society as a whole? These questions are more than abstract philosophical issues: as events in our world accelerate, each of us must make choices affecting both our own lives and those around us. And agreement about human nature and freedom is far from unanimous – every major political and religious movement has answered these questions in their own, often divergent ways.

In this illuminating work, from which readers can draw insights for their own lives, the author poses the central question of what it is to be fully human. Beginning with the Renaissance, he surveys primary sources for such seemingly contradictory approaches as Marxist Humanism (Marx, Engels, etc.), Christian Humanism (Maritain), and Existentialist Humanism (Sartre), as well as critical voices (Heidegger, Lévi-Strauss, Foucault), concluding with recent proposals including Gorbachev's perestroika, Viktor Frankl's focus on meaning and Mario Rodríguez Cobos (Silo) and New Humanism, all of which point to the need for a new and universal humanism that must be, more than an idea or a philosophy, a *human attitude,* capable of bringing people together while respecting their diversity.

April, 1997   *Translated by Andrew Hurley*
Philosophy/History   *222 pp, 5 .5 X 8.25*
$11.95 Softcover   *ISBN 1-878977-18-0*

Tales for Heart and Mind: The Guided Experiences, A Storybook for Grownups by Silo

Recipient of a 1994 Benjamin Franklin Book Award, this collection of twenty-one sage and lively tales invites the reader into a playful theater of life. Timeless yet contemporary, this illustrated large-format storybook for grownups is of dual interest, both entertaining and useful in bringing personal peace and resolution. Over 40 original drawings by Joseph Berry.

James Michener called it "...a unique contribution to the mix of history, fable, racial memories and contemporary experience. [Silo's] passages – short stories, scenes, prose poems – tantalize the mind and generate understandings." *Publishers Weekly* comments that these stories "...speak meaningfully to our daily predicaments..." *Clarín,* Buenos Aires' largest newspaper says "...underlying these apparently simple stories are deeper meanings fed by psychological insights and literary roots ranging from Lewis Carroll to Jung, Dante, Shakespeare, the Tarot, and the *Popol-Vuh*...overcoming the way in which competition and compartmentalization in today's world separate us from ourselves."

Fiction/Storytelling   *160 pages, Illustrated 8 x 10*
$18 Hardcover Gift Edition   *ISBN 1-878977-15-6*

Spoken Word Audio of Tales for Heart and Mind

Finally – a storybook for grownups. Rediscover the timeless literary and human experience of listening to stories read aloud. Enter this playful theater as the protagonist, seeing events in your life unfold amid the settings of these enchanting and useful stories that bring you peace and insight. Accompanied by music and a useful companion to the illustrated book. Digitally mastered in stereo.

Spoken Word Audio   *3 Audio Volumes*
7 stories each, 60-70 min.   *Each Volume $9.95 cassette*
ISBN Vol. I: 1-878977-25-3,   Coming: Vol. II: 25-1, Vol. III: 28-8

Silo: Obras Completas, Volumen I

The first volume of the complete works of Silo, one of the most profound and provocative authors of our time. Five unabridged works in the original Spanish including *Humanizar la Tierra* (*La Mirada Interna, El Paisaje Interno, El Paisaje Humano*), *Experiencias Guiadas* (translated in *Tales for Heart and Mind*), *Contribuciones al Pensamiento, Mitos Raíces Universales, El Día del León Alado, Cartas a mis amigos sobre la crisis social y personal en el momento actual* (eight letters in this volume; all ten letters translated in *Letters to My Friends*).

Literatura / Filosofía / Mitología   *504 pages, 5 1/2 X 8 1/2*
$16.95 Quality Softcover   *ISBN 1-878977-24-5*

Self Liberation by Luis Ammann

The original 1981 edition of this classic title explains in clear language a body of thought that makes human behavior and one's own life understandable in today's world. Closely integrates clear, simple ideas with practical exercises addressing both personal and social change. This original out-of-print first edition is available only through this catalog. Revised edition forthcoming.

Psychology   *176 pages, 7 x 10*
$8.95 Softcover   *Original Edition*

Booklets and Video

"The Crisis of Traditional Humanism and Remarks on New Humanism" by Salvatore Puledda

A penetrating examination of the difficulties of traditional humanisms and today's conception of the human being as a "biochemical machine," plus remarks on New Humanism. Presented in a talk by the author of *On Being Human*.

$3 postpaid, 28 pgs.   *5 1/2 X 8 1/4, Booklet Number One*

"Overcoming Social and Personal Crisis in Today's World" by Silo

A lucid framing of the task and role of New Humanism in contemporary life, presented in a talk by Silo on the publication of his work *Letters to My Friends: On Social and Personal Crisis in Today's World*.

$3 postpaid, 32 pgs.   *5 1/2 X 8 1/4, Booklet Number Two*

"In the Blink of an Eye" by Daniel Zuckerbrot

An award-winning (Chicago Film Festival, 1996 Cindy Award) very short subject that captures the acceleration of time in today's world and the feeling or sensation this produces within us. An interesting tool for personal reflection.

$8   *VHS, 5 minutes running time*

Forthcoming Titles in the New Humanism Series

Silo Speaks

A wide-ranging record of the thought of Mario Rodríguez Cobos, Silo, one of Latin America's most profound and provocative authors. A compilation of more than 20 talks covering almost 30 years of public life including speeches at rallies, talks upon the publication of his books, and other addresses. *Public Affairs/Humanism*

Humanism in Different Cultures
by the World Center for Humanist Studies

A collection of essays outlining humanist expressions in various cultures. Includes humanist contributions from Islamic, Chinese, Ibero-American, Jewish, and Native American cultures.
History / Humanism

Dictionary of New Humanism, edited by Silo

The first edition of this dictionary, which will be expanded, aspires to shed light on the various uses and meanings of the word humanism and associated terms, with emphasis on New Humanism as a specific form of humanism. *Reference/Humanism*

Morphology: Signs, Symbols, and Allegories in Human Life
by José Caballero

An accessible work for non-specialists analyzing the principal signs and symbols of human history and many cultures. Highlights habitually overlooked roles such forms play in our lives, not only through signs and conventions but also through symbols and allegories. A must for the visual arts. *Morphology / Art / Psychology*

Day of the Winged Lion and Other Stories by Silo

Awarded the *Nuove Lettere* International Prize for Poetry and Literature from the Istituto Italiano di Cultura and the journal *Nuove Lettere* (in Italian translation). Imaginative, ironic, and powerful stories in Silo's spare, contemporary prose. In contrast to what is usual for the fantastic genre, rather than carrying us into the world of dreams, these stories subtly bring us back to what is fundamental in life. Silo's stories never fail to illuminate, amuse, and provoke the reader's thinking in fresh directions. *Fantasy / Science Fiction*

50 Ways to Humanize Your Neighborhood
by Daniel Zuckerbrot and Paul Tooby

A step-by-step guide to building human communication in your own neighborhood. Emphasizes uniting people as human beings in addressing common needs while respecting their differences. Examples of successful programs in many countries. *Social Action*

Humanize the Earth, A Trilogy: The Inner Look, The Inner Landscape, The Human Landscape by Silo

This beautiful and profound book expresses in simple poetic prose a humanist approach to life that is finding increasing resonance in today's world. Ranges broadly from the larger questions of human existence to the particulars of daily life. *Philosophy / Literature*

Configuring a Personal Inner Guide by Pia Figuroa

An inspiring and useful account of developing often-overlooked inner resources for finding the kindness, wisdom, and strength that are more than ever necessary in contemporary life.

Contributions to Thought by Silo

Two philosophical essays, the first on the human mind, how thought is represented and the central role of the image; the second on how time and history are central and intrinsic parts of human existence. *Philosophy*

The Tokarev Report by Salvatore Puledda

A gripping multi-level story in both the book itself and the role it may have played in averting nuclear war in the '80s. Prescient in its predictions of what is now taking place in Eastern Europe and the former Soviet Union. Follows the protagonist Yuri Tokarev on an exotic world journey as he attempts to trace the source of the strange mental phenomena that are intensifying in the populations of many countries, for which conventional science can offer no coherent rational explanation. *Fantasy / Science Fiction*

Universal Root Myths by Silo

An intriguing and thorough compilation of the universal myths that recur across various cultures. Based entirely on the original texts, faithfully and skillfully completed where gaps exist, preserving the voice of the original. *Mythology*

About the Authors

Luis Ammann was born in Argentina in 1942. In 1969 he joined the research group that gave shape to the Self Liberation system and other still unpublished works that form a significant contribution to the science of psychology and an interesting alternative to traditional lines of thought. A founding member of the Humanist Party in Argentina, he continues to work on expressions of contemporary humanism that combine personal and social change. He lives in Argentina with his wife and son.

José Caballero was born in Spain in 1952. Following his education, he pursued his talents as an illustrator and graphic artist. For more than a decade he dedicated himself to this study of morphology, from an analysis of the principal signs and symbols used throughout history to documenting the meaning, interpretation, and function of the symbols and allegories employed in diverse human cultures as well as their role in the inner and outer life of the individual. He lives in Madrid with his wife and children.

Pia Figueroa was born in Chile in 1953. A founding member of the Humanist Party of Chile, she served as Undersecretary of State for the Environment in Chile's first democratically elected government since the 1973 coup. She is currently working on a model of neighborhood development that bridges people's differences while respecting their diversity. She lives in Santiago with her husband and two children.

Salvatore Puledda was born in Rome in 1943. Educated in Italy and the United States, he received his doctorate in Chemistry from the University of Rome. He has authored approximately fifty scientific papers on atmospheric pollution and environmental health while maintaining an active interest in the social consequences of applications of science and technology, which he studied with Herbert Marcuse. He lives in Rome with his wife and daughter.

Mario Rodríguez Cobos, pen name Silo, was born in Argentina in 1938. In October of 1993 he received an honorary doctorate from the Russian National Academy of Sciences for the contributions of his writings to humanity's efforts to face the dramatic changes in today's world. An important voice in New Humanism, his constructive efforts against violence in a dehumanized society and coherent proposals for combining personal and social change have had important influence on organizations with a humanist, nonviolent, and ecological approach to social change. He lives with his wife and two sons in Argentina.

Daniel Zuckerbrot was born in Pennsylvania in 1954. As a producer of documentary films at the CBC, his award-winning films form a notable contribution to education and understanding in the acclaimed "Nature of Things" series. He lives with his wife and two children in Toronto.

Order Information for the *New Humanism Series*

Available at bookstores or for a Catalog from the publisher:
Latitude Press • P.O. Box 231516 • Encinitas, CA 92023-1516
800-LATITUDE (528-4883) • Fax 619-632-6359
73250.574@compuserve.com • www.latitudepress.com

Quantity   Title   Each   Total

_____

_____

_____

_____

_____

_____

Subtotal _____

California orders include sales tax _____

Shipping and Handling _____

Total Enclosed _____

Payment: Check or Credit card in US funds (Visa or Mastercard, include card number, expiration date, name on card).

Name_____

Address_____

City, State, Zip/PC _____

Phone_____

Email_____

Shipping and Handling: USA: $3.00 first book (Canada & Mexico $5) plus $2 per additional book. Outside USA: $12 plus $8 per additional book, by Air only. Postpaid items: Include $2 for Canada or $5 for other countries. Information subject to change without notice.